Alexander McKenzie

The Divine Force in the Life of the World

Vol. 1

Alexander McKenzie

The Divine Force in the Life of the World
Vol. 1

ISBN/EAN: 9783337780173

Printed in Europe, USA, Canada, Australia, Japan

Cover: Foto ©Lupo / pixelio.de

More available books at **www.hansebooks.com**

The Divine Force in the Life of the World

[Lowell Institute Lectures]

By

Alexander McKenzie

Author of
"A Door Opened," "Christ Himself," "Some Things Abroad," "Cambridge Sermons"

Lamson, Wolffe and Company
Boston, New York, London
MDCCCXCVIII

TO MY WIFE
WHOSE COUNSEL AND ENCOURAGEMENT ARE MY CONTINUAL HELP

PREFACE

The contents of this book were recently given as a course of lectures before the Lowell Institute. They are now published by the request and advice of many persons whose judgment is with authority. No change has been made in the substance of the lectures, and very little in their form. Some passages which were omitted in the reading are now printed in their place, and here and there a sentence has been added.

The purpose of the book will be evident to any one who reads it. I claim no novelty for this; but I cannot too strongly assert my conviction of the profound importance of the one truth which has controlled me from the beginning of the pages, which I offer for the cheer and comfort of the serious days in which we are living.

Alexander McKenzie.

The First Church in Cambridge,
October, 1898.

CONTENTS

		PAGE
I.	The Creation and Man	1
II.	The Course of Man in the Oldest Literature	51
III.	The Son of Man in early Literature	115
IV.	The Purpose and Method of Christ	165
V.	The Cause of Christ in the Hands of Men	219
VI.	The Christian Forces	277
	Index	327

I

THE CREATION AND MAN

THE CREATION AND MAN

It was by a somewhat singular process of self-restraint that one whose life had been that of a parish minister undertook to treat the themes of religion without preaching; to separate them from feeling and appeal, from personal experience and desire, and to regard them simply as vital and interesting truths. Yet this is possible. It is certainly necessary, lest the truths of religion should become too closely identified with our own thought and habit of thinking; with advantages which we propose to derive from them; with cherished ideas and vested interests; with institutions and constitutions to which, in our suggestive phrase, we "belong."

While in its most serious meaning religion is related to experience, if it is trustworthy we should be able to stand on the outside of it, and to examine it, and the evidences which attend it, in the light of reason and conscience, of spiritual thought, of history, of influence, and with the highest intellectual and ethical honesty. If it appeals to faith, as it must do because of its relation to the unseen, it is a faith which rests on intelligence, and can justify itself with truth.

It is proposed to consider certain elements of religion; and not the forms which have been given to them. A truth, if it remains among men, finds a body formed around it, with members and organs, with structure and weight. The form has its honor and its use. But it may come to pass that this is more conspicuous than the truth which is in it, which must shine through it, with its light, perhaps, colored and diverted on the way; as a ray from the sun is shattered by the prism which is thrust in its path. Yet it should not be very hard to find the truth and to regard it by itself. The universal interest in that which may be termed religion is promising. The gathering of materials belonging to it will be followed by the construction of the Temple. It is the usual order, though not invariable in this kind of building. If I may cite an ancient writer, whose name I do not know, there are signs which suggest "the removing of those things that are shaken, as of things that have been made, that those things which are not shaken may remain."

Others have spoken and written upon the various departments of religious thought and life, and their words are with us, rich in learning, and the more instructive because their breadth permitted depth. It were as dull as it would be useless for me to attempt to do again what has been done well. It were better that I should recognize what has been said, and make use of it so far as it will assist my design. As I look toward the westering sun, whose slant beams fall on many years which have been spent among these things that we have in mind, I hold it for myself, and for those who trust me, to be well determined that there is a permanent reality called religion; with spirit and form, with word and life; and that without extraordinary effort thoughtful men and women can have it, and rejoice in it. This must certainly be so, if there is the reality. For in its nature religion must be universal, and hence in its elements readily comprehended. It is not, in its principles, subject to our control. It expresses the true relation of man to God, and that we have to learn and accept and employ. It is given to us as the light is, and cannot itself be changed in our hands.

When we have gone beyond the first principles there is room for diversity of belief and statement, and no one can complain that the room has not been occupied. There is a variety of opinions, reaching as far as thought can go; affected by lands and times and conditions, by mental traits and desires, and appalling in character and amount. Can we get away far enough to be free from conditions, and find the comfort which is for those who live "in the familiar thought of the eternal years"?

I shall refer from time to time to the earliest chapters of the Bible. Let me say once for all that I do this, not because they are in the Bible, but because they are our oldest literature, which entitles them to respect; and they give a concise and connected account of the times of which we have no better record. They furnish an excellent statement of early events. They assert a further claim upon our regard, but that I shall not press.

There is a point at which, with full consent, our thought begins. I like the superb organ tones of those primal words of the primal book, "In the beginning, God." There reason and imagination rest. The mind may wish to venture on, but this is the last solid ground. Shall we meet there, and, unable to go farther north, come down into the world of to-day?

I see the difficulty of this method. It would seem easier to start from our streets and ascend until we come to God in his solitude. But is it not best to begin with the simple, and is not God clearer than the world; concealed, confused, contradictory to us who are in the midst of it, and whirling around with it? It is better to begin in the mystery than to end in it. The world is plainer when we stand with God and look upon it than is God when we stand in the world and lift our eyes to Him. We cannot know Him perfectly; but the knowledge to which we can attain illumines the earth. Mysteries are merely truths which are not yet disclosed, and they are opened before us in the light of his presence.

Religion in any intelligent use of the term must confess a supreme mind and will, which can be known and ought to be obeyed. It is more than knowledge and obedience, for its home is in the deepest nature of man, where in its allegiance to the true and its devotion to the right it governs the life. We seem to be coming toward a serviceable agreement concerning these things. A prominent teacher of philosophy, not identified with the common religious thought, closed an address not long ago with the remark, "I am certainly disposed to insist that what the faith of our fathers has genuinely meant by God is identical with the inevitable outcome of a reflective philosophy."

Religion is in the highest sense personal, for it is the worship, the loyalty, of the spirit who is man, responding to the divinity of the spirit who is God. If we ask what upon our side is the source of religion and the religious idea, the answer is prepared. They have their source within the life of man, and are inseparable from it. For the life must be lower than it has anywhere been found to be devoid of the principle of religion. But what is the source of the life of man which brings religion within it? The answer again is obvious. At the first, before all things, or ever creation had issued into the void of space, was the Eternal, the Almighty. "In the beginning, God." I do not know when they were first written, or spoken, or thought, those four words. They come from a realm into which no discoverer has penetrated. They keep their place in our thought because they are true. They are at the opening of the oldest book in use. It is accounted a book of religion, but that should not lessen its authority. There are the words, with unrecorded centuries upon them. It is of more than ordinary interest, to think of a man whose name and land we do not know, of whom we have no sign but in these syllables and the sentences which follow them, finding his way into his undetermined past, and telling to his children, and through them to the world, this simple, massive truth, and relating the deeds which in grandeur stand within it. The first chapter of the Book needs no name to give it majesty. Whence it came no one can tell.

Here I might rest, so far as this is concerned. If I add a fifth word, the universe starts into being: . . . "In the beginning God created." Here an entirely new word appears, and a new fact. Language and history are enriched in one event. Science receives a stupendous endowment. Alone in his eternity He dwelt and all life was his. It is beyond our thought, but not so far beyond as would be the denial of it. We willingly allow our thought to flow out to the Eternal and there to rest among the mysteries which do not weary us. What resources for companionship the Creator had in his own being we need not now inquire. From the fellowship in our own nature we infer with confidence of reasoning the perfect fellowship within his infinite being, and of this many things have been written. I am concerned here only with the presence of the life, whose reality is the earliest truth. By his will, through his power, He made that to be which was not, and could not otherwise become. "The Universal Cause, itself uncaused," by its living will summoned creation.

He must have delighted to create. How readily we use the new word, failing to think of the fathomless mysteries which it contains! Creation! Who shall describe it? Its results we perceive; but by what process have they come? Creation is not the combining of materials, for there were no materials. It is not the erection of a building, or the construction of a mechanism. Creation is the outreaching of energy, thought, will, life, into forms which they had not known. But when and how did this come to pass? With the advance of our knowledge this constantly recurring question is not more easily answered. We have many things relating to the world, and the worlds, and their life, but they have kept this secret. If we no longer imagine the Almighty upon some day which is a little beyond our calendar making a universe and sending it on its course; if we cherish the later announcement that it was by almost interminable processes that the universe was produced, — the nebular dust with no discoverable motion gathering itself into stars, and the jetsam and flotsam of chaos stretching themselves in unmeasured planes to make the earth, — still the time, and the way, refuse to declare themselves. But earth and sky, and air and sea, confess the divine hand that made them, and with their thousand voices utter their praise.

I have fallen into the old way in saying the

divine hand. They were not hand-made. But the language has very high authority and is convenient. It is hard to describe what no one has ever thoroughly told.

"In the beginning, God." He was all the life. Religion and science are in accord. Many have spoken of life. The last official utterance which has come to my notice was made by one who is, I suppose, as well entitled to speak as any one in the world. In the distinguished medical congress in Moscow last year Professor Virchow, of Berlin, gave an address upon "The Continuity of Life." "Life," he said, "had no other origin than from Life itself, and this is one of the truths which the labors of the pathologist and biologist of the present century have established beyond the possibility of doubt." We knew that before. But it is well to hear it again from time to time. He thought it necessary to call it to the minds of the hundreds of physicians who had flocked to the Kremlin. He closed with the hope "that the final mystery of life might be solved through similar studies. It is in their laboratory that the key will be forged which shall unlock the door which still holds us back from full knowledge of the processes of life." I cannot think there is the remote probability that this learning will ever be acquired. Meantime we shall continue to live.

We are confirmed in our knowledge of the one origin of life. In this is our hope, nor does science "waft us home the message of despair." "In Him was life." He was the life. In that life, with it, of it, for it, He created. The purpose to create was in the beginning, an eternal thought. In that sense creation was eternal, for his purposes do not change. It could then, in a large measure, have its value for Him. His idea was the reality. It is easiest to retain the ordinary conception and to think of the creation as an event in time.

From another point of view it has been reasoned in this way: God is spirit, and it is the essence of spirit to manifest itself; and creation "is the eternal self-revelation of God." He was not dependent upon it, yet creation was certain to come. At any rate, its coming was reasonable and desirable. To have this shut up in his intention could not have been permanent; for, in the first place, creation was to be for others also; and, again, it was to be his delight to call the others into being, that they might enjoy the earth and the heavens, and receive his love which needed true hearts for its home, and return it in their love which must needs be the free and personal offering of a real soul. The Almighty, as it were, went beyond Himself. The terms are sadly inaccurate — his thought reached away, his will carried his life out, and gave it larger being and form. What the first forms were is of little consequence in comparison with the fact that they were; that the created was in the presence of the eternal. It is for the students of life and form to find out what this beginning was, and to tell us who are busy with other things. "If the whole body were an eye, where were the hearing?" Science has been tardy, but it has come to our help at last. We shall not let it go till it has blessed us, and its full blessing no one of us shall see. Science is prophet and psalmist, proclaiming truth, and teaching us to rejoice and be glad in it. I believe it has been called the handmaid of religion. The term is not accurate. Religion has no handmaid. It is the associate, the friend, of religion. They work for one end — the knowledge of God, to the intent that He may be worshipped. Science without religion lacks its true and highest purpose. Religion without science is likely to be sentiment, and not virtue.

It is now evident that the first created forms were simple. There was a force working for their enlargement and continuation. What was needed was a starting; a living seed, which in the ages that were plentiful might be made a tree, a grove, a forest. We find it difficult to see the beginning. It would have been difficult then to see the end. Indeed, we do not see it now. But the result was to be accomplished, and not by some power made inherent in things. This which had been made had not been cast off in its infancy, to live if it could. The divine life was to continue to be its life. The shears did not come near the thread. "That cruel Atropos" was not yet invented. The one life was to be the reason and ground of its existence. The presence of the Creator was to be in all things. He could not be identified with them. They were not God. He could withdraw his life and care, and they would vanish away. They were not so much as the form or the raiment of the Creator. They were his works, and He was before them, in the strength and glory of eternal being. They could be multiplied without limit. Other things might be set in their places. But in and after all changes He would remain the same, administering his "undisturbed affairs." He was not all in the things he had made, restricted by them, embodied in their bounds. If I may vary the image, the ocean is in every bay and harbor along the coast. This is the only and sufficient ground of their being. If the ocean should withdraw, they would all cease to be. The tides of the ocean are felt on the shore. It is a poor illustration.

The ocean is in the harbors, but is not dependent upon them. They are utterly dependent upon the ocean. It wears away the shore and makes new harbors for itself, but it does not imprison its waters. The Atlantic rolls to-night about Minot's Ledge, but it is three thousand miles to Fastnet Rock, and the ocean reaches all the way. No meridian makes a mark upon its waves. So is it with the divine life. It is the ocean flowing into the bays. We must recognize "an omnipresent energy, which is none other than the living God." "The one eternal and ultimate reality is the absolute life of God."

We are reminded of the youth of our present views of the creating of the world when we find a man as recent as Plato describing the disorder of sensible things, and the Deity as making each thing harmonize with itself and with other things, and then out of them constructing the universe. We are not troubled by this simplicity. After all there is the Deity. If we have Him, "sensible things" come readily, and are obedient. No one has yet traced the intermediate steps between the Eternal and the world as we have seen it. But the main facts are clear, and it is these which impress us. We are driven to the use of our own language when we speak of God, and the language is not adapted to such service. Yet it does its best; and if we have imagination, and are at liberty, the assistance is real. It is in this spirit I hazard the remark, that it was a supreme moment with the Almighty when He gave to his eternal design the form which was named creation. It was the free, glad, ready outworking of his wisdom and power. We can almost think his delight when for the first time " the morning stars sang together, and all the sons of God shouted for joy;" and the content with which He "saw everything that He had made, and, behold, it was very good." Life is generous, munificent. It gives itself. He was generosity, for He was love; and this became creation. The divine thought rejoiced when it was literally born into the world. We connect the Creator and creation, and properly. Each is disclosed in the other. God is revealed in his works, and the meaning of the works is found in Him. We know nothing completely, but we nurse the incompleteness of our knowledge when we sever it from that to which it is vitally united, and regard it altogether by itself. The heavens declare the glory of God and God declares the glory of the heavens. They have their real value in the shining through them of his light. Nature is a convenient and elastic term, and all that it contains deserves our notice. But in its connection with the unseen, divine original it has its permanent meaning. It has been honored in many ways; but the most graceful tribute ever paid to it is at the opening of the earliest record, where in a single brief sentence, without a break, the Eternal stands with his works. His glory reaches over, and draws the worlds to itself and holds them there. Not even a comma separates God and the created. "In the beginning God created the heaven and the earth." Astronomy, Geology, the whole science of nature has never written a more majestic line. "In the beginning God created the heaven and the earth." These are the words of the record which throughout is in accord with them. The account is unparalleled for the combining of scientific and religious truth; or, rather, for stating religion in the terms of science and giving to science the spirit of religion. In this it differs essentially from all other ancient stories of creation.

Many writings which have come to be associated with it maintain this fellowship between God and his works. They are under his control, are used in his service, are clothed with his power. His truth is continually illustrated by means of his works. Not poets only, prophets, apostles, join God and his works in their thoughts. The great Teacher made all things, even the grass at his feet, explain the ways of God. He made the facts of nature illustrate and assist the truths of human life. He pointed out the "natural law in the spiritual world." Thus we have our book of religion and it is a book of nature. The heavens bend over its pages, the ocean rolls around them, and the fields bloom with providence. Mountains and hills tower above the lines, and rivers run through them; among them rise trees in whose branches birds build their nests. Trace these all back, from book to book, from age to age, and you come at length, you are glad to come, to those earliest words, so compact with meaning, so rich with information, so full of scientific truth,— the august, lasting verities of the universe.

I do not propose to read the weighty statements which follow that upon which I have delayed. For me there is a wonderful charm in the first pages of the first book. So far as I am acquainted with literature there is nothing to compare with them in the magnificence of their themes and the grandeur of their treatment, and the tremendous hold they get on thought and life. I have given to the record no name. I have asserted no claim for it, except that it is a writing, and that it has reached us from an illimitable past. Some one made it. There is no reason to question his belief that he was telling the truth. Whence he gained his knowledge and assurance he does not tell. His sentences are strong and clear, and it is very remarkable that they so well anticipate what could not be known by observation for a great many centuries. I think there is nothing in the history of thought more surprising than the general agreement of our later scientific knowledge, acquired by long and progressive study, with the condensed statements of this man to whom all that we name science was unknown, undreamed. The vexed question how Shakespeare could have written the plays which bear his name is nothing compared with the question how this man, who did not even put his name to his work, could have written the first chapter of the book "commonly called Genesis." To ascribe the book to Moses does nothing to resolve the matter, for the account itself is evidently from a much earlier time. To call it tradition is of no service, for tradition is the thought of men as really as if it were written. And where did the tradition come from? No system of ancient cosmogony can be compared with this in value, as this has been determined in recent years. I am not using the account to teach either science or religion, but as an excellent statement of events which antedate history. It could not well be improved for substantial accuracy, for simplicity, directness, reverence, modesty, and the poetic beauty and grace which at once enlist and inspire the imagination. The old record was not made for a text-book in natural history. It was to present God as the Creator of all things, and this it does. It has been placed at the opening of a series of books whose design is to show the ways of God with men. It does efficiently what it was made to do. But beyond this we have a remarkable agreement with our later knowledge, in the thought of the Creator, the progress of events, the advance from the simple to the complex, from lower to higher forms, by indeterminate periods. It is not of vital importance that it should be in close and perfect agreement with all which is now known. If our knowledge were more complete, I think the coincidence would be even more astounding than it is now.

There are moments which are of startling interest. I had these things in mind when a few weeks ago I met on the street a very eminent geologist, the head of a scientific school, who told me as the result of his study that he believed the first living creature was a fish. Others have reached the same conclusion, but it came to me then with special force. I opened my Bible as quickly as I could, and found that a man far away in the wilderness of the ages had written as the first words in his catalogue of living things, "And God said, Let the waters bring forth abundantly the moving creature that hath life." Was that a lucky guess, or a flash of genius, or the fortunate achievement of a poetic imagination? Who was this peerless man? Where is his successor? Our respect for Adam is variable. But for this man, who traces day by day, age by age, the forming of the heavens, the building of the earth, the peopling them, by slow gradation, with fish that swim, and birds that fly, and cattle that roam the meadows, — who can have less than a proud admiration for him? What else of his period has lasted? Yet here are the words that come from antiquity, once written, once spoken, and never lost; which we read in the light of to-day and do not care to change; which expand under our eyes, but are never affrighted by our search. They are like notes upon the sheet, whose melody has not been discovered until now, when men whose brain and fingers are full of music wake the silence into sound.

There are other separated accounts of the former things. They serve to mark the sublimity of this. They resemble one another, and all reach into a time when things were not as we behold them. They find a beginning, and the stages of advance, and at times they give us the story of creation in attractive forms. But they do not commend themselves to our judgment. They do not begin with the Creator. Usually they start with chaos, out of which emerge even the gods. With discordant beginnings, the course and the meaning of nature could not be the same.

Yet the other systems are of interest. But they are complex, mechanical, making much of the apparatus for constructing worlds. They are in bold contrast with the dignity and simplicity and quietness which pervade the description which comes to us from the Hebrews. The account which we have deserves the more praise, if, besides being formed, it has kept the integrity of its life when all besides has suffered change.

One is almost compelled, and quite permitted, to think that this account of events which no man saw had a divine origin, and was preserved and transmitted under special care.

I do not wish to claim too much for one man, as if he alone possessed this archaic information which, by another route, has now reached us. Probably there was a common body of tradition, or belief, among the peoples of Western Asia. If this is so, it was given to the writer, or writers, of the first chapters of Genesis to receive the tradition, to know its value, to separate from it the degrading ideas which are found in other systems,

— polytheism, nature-worship, and all which belonged with them, — and to transmit the knowledge in a form worthy of its character. In this the Creator is before all things, and He is to be worshipped, and not the works which He has made. The simple, spiritual, divine tone pervading the record is unexampled in those times, unsurpassed in any time. No one will understand me to say that these writers had any idea of that we call science; any intuitions of our discoveries, and foregleams of our theories. But they knew that God was first, and that He created, and that life ascended to the highest form they knew, which is the highest form we know. We are not able elsewhere to reach so far into the past. We read the story of nature in the rocks, turning the leaves and spelling out the words. But the broken record is legible only about "half way down in the history of organic events," and it is not likely that the earlier pages will be recovered. An eminent naturalist states it in this way: "The dead past has not only buried its dead, but has quite effaced the burial places."

Our account of the creation is remarkable, also, for what it does not say. Compare the traditions, still preserved in books of stone, which made the learning of other peoples, only to admire the clearness and reasonableness of these unstudied annals. Of method nothing is detected. Order is declared with surprising intelligence, but no bounds are set around the working of the Eternal, who has the ages in his keeping, with a thousand years, a thousand centuries, for a day.

It has been left for men to find out the ways of the Creator, and to study his works; to match life with life, and age with age; to search the rocks and bring their hidden treasures to the light; to explore the heavens and learn how stars and suns were made; how the bands of Orion were woven and the sweet influences of the Pleiades are distilled. The argument from design to the Designer has been contested, but the principle survives. Might it not be made to include the obscurities among which we live, which give to the mind good exercise and fine training? The pearl may have been placed at the bottom of the sea to give the diver the excitement of plunging into the deep and rising with his prize. There is thoughtfulness in leaving the world's making unwritten, save in its deep lines, that we might have the pleasure of finding it out; hunting its meanings and methods, and profiting by the mental athletics. What privation it would have been to discovery and research, if the written account had been complete! If getting truth is better even than having it, the world is well adjusted to our advantage. It is to the credit of scientific and philosophic study that its results are so liberally confirmed by the words of strange origin which begin our literature. Learning is far from complete, as we gratefully confess; but the grand truths which it now presents with enlarging enterprise have high sanction in the laden sentences which so long revealed and so long concealed the heaven and the earth. It is a large world which lies about us; which has come forth from those far-off events. I have not tried to count them, but I have been told there are now upon this globe a million, or a million and a half, species of animals and plants, — the margin is liberal, — and that there have been a hundred times as many, in inconceivable variety. We look up, and millions of suns shine in the firmament we call our own, and beyond this are thousands of firmaments with their bright worlds moving in grandeur and splendor, in order and quietness, by a force no optic glass can discover, while the careless centuries watch their flight. We see so little! We know so little! There are both wit and wisdom in the comment of Cardinal Baronius: "The intention of Holy Scripture is to teach us how to go to heaven, and not how the heavens go." We cannot bring creation into the terms which describe our own work. Yet it is instructive to find the laws which rule in lesser matters prevailing in the larger. Even analogy and similitude have their value. It was interesting to have one who had been President of Harvard College argue for the reasonableness of miracles from the law of the parabola; and to hear our American mathematician say that "the laws of mathematics are but the expression of the thoughts of God;" and that the mathematician must cling to "the spiritual view of the origin of the universe." It was a Christian who wrote, "There is one Lawgiver." The beginning of all is found in the strong lines which are the record of creation, with the recurring refrain which marks the periods which have no boundary lines, "And there was evening, and there was morning, one day."

But the crown of creation we have not yet reached. We have kept in the order of nature. A few words complete the history we have admired. It is a moment for stillness. The earth stretches around us. The stars are over us. The fishes range the seas. The birds are in the air. Life moves silently in its work. There is no one here to think of this, and to enjoy it, on all the hills, over all the fields. It is virtually an untenanted world; not deserted, but never inhabited. Rest for a moment, and think on the first man whose foot pressed the earth, whose eye looked through the trees. Human history has felt no words more eventful than these: "And God created man in his own image." Where did the writer we are coming to trust learn that? Where he learned the things he had told before. If he had written more fully! Perhaps his hand was held, and not impelled as some have imagined. It is certain that he was nearer our own time in his thought than most have been in the years between us. There is a modern rather than a mediæval tone in his entire narrative. It is steadily progressive, and there are no breaks in it. God in the beginning. Light, earth, sea; seed, grass, trees; sun, moon, stars; living, moving creatures in the sea, and on the land, and above the earth, — it reads like a family history; and the increasing life reaches its consummation in man. The love which He is called for man, for some one to be loved; for one to enjoy life and delight in God.

It is natural to suppose there was a relationship among all things which had received life from the one source of life. The distinct periods, whose limit our author appears not to have known, would give time for the life to take on its higher forms, on its way to the highest. What are the stages for, unless it were this? "There was evening and there was morning, one day. And there was evening and there was morning, a second day." The original record has a kindly look toward the scientific beliefs which now prevail. If the ancient annalist knows how long we have been in reaching them, I am not at all sure but he smiles at our laggard ways. The connection of man on his physical side with the world he lives in and with other forms of life seems to be demonstrated. Those who have given the most attention to this matter, and are the best qualified to have an opinion, are agreed that this is true. We are indebted to them for the pains they have taken to make us intelligent concerning ourselves and our past. They startled us at first, and there seemed to be reason for alarm. But that is over; and the principle, variously modified and defined, appears to be established among thoughtful men. This has come about rapidly enough. It is wise to be careful, that is, conservative, in affairs of importance, especially those with which we are not familiar. If a discovery, or a new theory, has any virtue it will be willing to wait till its credentials can be examined. There is little danger at present that scientific discoveries will be kept waiting longer than is for their good. The things which have a right to live will live. There is no need of saying now — I am sorry there was ever need of saying

— that the new views to which I have alluded, which concern the life of men, do not in the least separate the world from God. If there is any difference to be imagined, it would appear that the continual presence of the Creator would be even more necessary through the gradual rise of man from a humble origin than in a sudden creation. "In the beginning God" is firmer than mountains and all hills, or "the great globe itself." "The living will" must endure, and move in all things. There are more things to be studied and known than before, but the truth we knew before remains. It is not all an open country traversed by wide roads. But the way is clearer than it was. The increase of our knowledge of God's ways should enlarge our confidence in Him.

There is in Genesis another account of the creation of man of which we know no more than of the first. Somewhere, at some time, by some one, it was believed, and told, and written, and at length placed beside the first. This writer did not describe creation in general. He may have seen the earlier description or tradition, or have heard of it. He began by saying that "the heaven and the earth were finished, and all the host of them." This lacks the grandeur of the other. Then he described the seventh day, the hallowed day of rest; the day made for man, who, even to this time, does not know the blessing that is in it. While in many things we have advanced, we have lost ground in regard to this. A few words of the first watering of the earth; and he wrote his account of the creation of the man. "And the Lord God formed," — that is much like the other, "God created," — "formed man of the dust of the ground," — the other writer had shown the dust, — " and breathed into his nostrils the breath of life; and man became a living soul." This may have been by one act, or by a long-continued bestowal of life. The important truth is that it was done, and a man was "a living soul;" not merely "a living soul," but one constituted by the breath or life of the Creator. Our fathers read this, and learned its principal truth — God made man. They knew that as well as we do. But how was the dust gathered up into the shape we bear? They did not know. If at this time any one knows, he is in hiding. The drawing by the vanished hand is so strong that it cannot be mistaken for portraiture. The story is well guarded. The meaning cannot be missed. I think there is nothing more daring and realistic than this. Indeed, I do not think of anything in all the books more bold and impressive. I cannot even try to imagine it, for the attempt to give it form would take from its sublimity. This is the daring picture which makes us silent. The Almighty pressed his lips against the nostrils of the man who was made of the dust of the ground, and breathed in his own breath, and man became "a living soul," a divine soul, with the breath of the Creator for its highest life. It is a picture, a sculpture, a description; but the one vital truth which cannot be missed or misinterpreted is this: the breath of God unchanged became the breath of man to whom it was given; man received life of the life of God. With this divine life he was a living soul. At that moment religion became possible. For the first time there was in the new earth a person whom God could love; upon whom He could lavish his love, in the blessedness of loving, and one who could respond with love. If it was a delight to make a world, it was much more a delight to make a man who could enjoy it. It was a new earth when a man had come to live in it, and a new heaven when he watched the courses of the stars. It was Godlike to make a man. Love imparts itself and needs a man to receive it. Love gives joy, and a man loved of God will live in joy, and love gives him being. Love is in the divine life, and in the life which is born of it, and by reason of his life of love man can live in the joy of God. Thus love interprets life at its beginning.

Here is the mystery of life. We have it, and do not know what it is. There are no words to make it clearer. Alone in its presence we are silenced. I recall an impressive hour long ago, when an eminent naturalist uncovered the heart of the smallest bird. It was only a description, but the listeners were hushed as in worship, when the point of life was reached, revealed, unveiled. He parted the soft feathers, divided the delicate skin, opened the fragile framework; and there was the tiny heart, quietly beating through it all, its hidden forces working uncomplainingly, and holding the fair creature in being, with a skill and strength which all the cunning of the world could not imitate. It was a moment which has never lost its awe, when I saw the life of the Eternal throbbing in the heart of a humming-bird.

" And man became a living soul." This is literal. This is the important fact in creation, and is more easily understood than the events which surround it. The picture is simpler than the frame, and less showy. A very strong outline was drawn, and it was left for men of a later time to fill it in. Man was essentially allied with the earth, and with forms of life other than his own. He came by slow degrees from a very simple condition to the estate which he has held for the more recent centuries. This we are taught. He was also especially allied with God by his life, and particularly by his spiritual life, in which was his likeness to the Creator. What was the living soul which man became? By this he diverged from the living creatures around him, not disowning the relationship, but going away in paths of his own. It was the spiritual, to use the common term; the psychical, to use the word endeared to philosophy, which was to have control, and to be advanced. This was the man, who of his superior endowments was to have rule over his humble neighbors. This is the man for whom religion is possible.

I am especially desirous to emphasize the fact of life. I intend to do this all the way. It is the continuous thought of these pages. I might have entitled them One Life. In the beginning God. There was no life but God. Of his own life He created all that lived. The process of creation is not disclosed. In its nature it is "unthinkable." Some things are known which entered into it, and we may discover more. But we shall never comprehend creation. Things did not come forth from God, out of his own being, as fruit comes from a tree, as light from the sun. He created, and to all that lived He gave life; gave of his own life; or, if one thinks He gave an inferior life, that must have come from his life and have been like it. Only life gives life and there was no life but God. The vital point, then, the meaning, is this, that all things live by the life of God. We are startled, silenced, when we think that the oak and the ivy are one life; the Cedar of Lebanon and the "primrose by a river's brim;" the angel and the man; the archangel and the primrose! Of course life could be given, and was given, in higher and finer measure to a bird than to a bush; to a man than to the undiscovered form next below him. It was so very much more, and in a form so very much higher, that we may well call it a different life. I have wished to point out the one origin of life, and it is only as it relates to the life of man that we are now interested in it. There is his common, lower relationship, in being, existence, vitality. Then comes the higher, in thought, affection, will, and this is man's. Man, only man upon the earth, received directly the breath of the Eternal, and became a living soul, and was in the image and likeness of his Maker. He is man by virtue of this which allies him with God, not by that which gives him kindred with the life that is in the world. He received as the greater gift, the divine gift, which was to belong to him and to no other, the life of his Creator in its highest forms, spiritual and eternal. With this creation was completed. The life would need to be continued by Him who gave it. The divine gift of life would not be withdrawn. "The greatest contribution of modern science to human thought" is "the idea of the continuity of causation"— such is its own claim. Man's chief interest is in his new life which makes him the child of God. He may not disown the physical, but he must be constantly mindful of the spiritual life. He must look up. He must and can live in God, with thought, affection, purpose, conduct. If we think of God as immanent in all that lives, as regards man He is also transcendent, above, beyond, to be trusted and worshipped. The divine image must be steadily enlarged by thinking of God, conversing with Him, abiding under his influence, under the spell of his perfection, changing his desire into thought and deed, growing up "in all things into Him." No limit is to be discerned. "Godly" is an eternal word. It is the largest term which can be applied to man. To be "like Him" is the brightest vision of the New Testament. The reason of it is here, in this divine nature whereby a man is the child of God.

If I have wandered, I could not help it. Let us return. The breath of God is the true life of man. It is the Man. We call it the Soul. It were better to call it the Man. This, not less than this, is his distinctive character.

But when was the soul given? When did man begin? I turn to the old record which has proved its right to respect, but it does not commit itself, though a single word would have told us all the writer knew. It looks as if man was made of the dust, and that when this form was completed and endowed with common life, the living soul was in a single act breathed into it. This has been a common theory and has not been disproved. One purely scientific view sees in the soul a development of faculties which are recognized in the associated forms of life. It traces the process of the increase through the gradual appearance of spiritual life. But in this method there is opportunity for special additions of spiritual life at any time when the advance needs to be promoted, and the final result hastened. The belief that this was a distinct gift, added to all that was before it, is most in accord with the usual, continuous thought of men, and is naturally suggested by the narrative in Genesis. It is a fascinating study, but we have to do with it now only so far as to assure ourselves that man has a spiritual nature and that this is the gift of God. It is preëminently the life of God which is given only to man. It is a very old question, in what way man received his soul. Traducianism and Creationism are obsolete terms; but time was when they were names to fight for. Tertullian in the Western Church taught that the soul was once for all created and then by natural generation propagated with the body. Later, Augustine is found wrestling with the problem, and offended by Tertullian, turning to Jerome with a cry for light. " Teach me therefore, I beg you, what I should teach, what I should hold; and tell me if it be true that souls are made now and separately with each separate birth; . . . not all from the one soul, of the first man, but for every man a separate soul, like that one for Adam." The question was of importance by reason of its connection with other doctrines. Some held that for each individual a new soul was created and added to the body and its life. While still others, among them Origen and many in the Eastern Church, accepted the teaching of Plato, that human souls existed from the beginning, and through the birth of a child attained to their actual and personal life. I touch on these theories, which once were alive, that we may mark how little of novelty there is in the subjects of thought. " Whence came the soul we no more know than we know whence came the universe," is the remark of a teacher among us. The comparison is good. If we no more know, we no less know. Pardon me if I let another, at once philosopher and historian, tell us how, in his opinion, the case stands to-day. "The Platonic view of the soul, as a spiritual substance, an effluence from Godhood, which under certain conditions becomes incarnate in perishable forms of matter, is doubtless the view most consonant with the present state of our knowledge." "The Lord God breathed into his nostrils" is the primitive form of the more elegant expression, "an effluence from Godhood." Thus extremes meet; Genesis and to-day's philosophy. It is to the credit of both. Nothing since Plato, on the essential truth! All I am concerned with is that the soul life is from God and of God, and must always be related to Him; for He must sustain what He has bestowed. It was a most notable event when man, the being with a soul, appeared. May I let other masters speak? "The law of generational advance has in man undergone a sudden, indeed we may say a paroxysmal, alteration. . . . Our own species appears, from the point of view of its supreme success, not only most exceptional, but absolutely alone in the history of this sphere. . . . If to-morrow man should disappear from the planet, there is no reason to suppose that by any process of change a similar creature would be evolved, however long the animal kingdom continued to exist." The appearance of man opened "an entirely new chapter in the mysterious history of creation." "Not the production of any higher creature, but the perfecting of Humanity, is to be the glorious consummation of Nature's long and tedious work."

We cannot fail to notice the dignity of man in this light which is thrown upon his history; his increased worth by reason of the patient care which has advanced him in power; and the greater assurance that he will continue to be the object of the divine love, which will spare itself nothing that its work may be perfected. Man's history is prophecy. His experience is promise. His way leads upward. It doth not yet appear what he shall be. If any one is curious to know Man, I cannot point even now to anything more interesting than Plato's account of the soul. We recall it; that there is in man a divine nature of which God is the artificer, and that the junior gods were set to produce the mortal nature. The mortal body was made as if turned in a lathe, and in this was placed the immortal principle. The two natures had different parts of the body, with the neck as an isthmus between. It is strengthening to read his estimate of the real soul of man: "After the gods, the most divine of all his possessions as being most his own." The body is "according to nature ruled over by the ruling soul." The soul is a goddess, ever taking mind as an ally. The soul is to be honored "in the second rank after the gods." It is to have care in the present, and for all time. "The danger would appear to be dreadful if one should neglect it." This is wholesome reading. Is it true now as the wise old Greek wrote, that "Not one, so to say, honours his soul properly"? Let these serious words stay in our minds.

When we think who man is we are not surprised that in all places he is aware of God. What is this but that the undivided life of God, being in a man, is conscious of the life which has not been imparted, and is in God alone? Why should not the part feel the whole to which it belongs? We cannot be surprised at such expressions as "that immediate knowledge of God" which is our "normal state of existence," the "quickening, life-giving God-sense," and the almost divine talent for knowing God. The last biographer of Jonathan Edwards relates that "the God consciousness was the deepest substratum of his being," and that in him was "a divine and supernatural light." The same divine consciousness is ascribed to men like

Thomas Erskine and Frederick Maurice. The words of Dr. Mulford are vigorous and clear when he writes that "man is conscious of the being of God, and lives and acts in this consciousness, and the reality of the being of God so comes to him. The being of God is the primal truth. It is primitive in human thought; there is nothing before it, nor apart from it, from which it is to be derived. Thus the being of God has not its foundation in the life of humanity, but humanity has its foundation in the life of God." I venture to like my own way of stating it, crude and formal as it is; the portion of the life of God which is in a man is conscious of the whole life in which it belongs.

It is true, as we are told with wearisome and perhaps needless repetition, that we are not able to conceive absolute being with an approach to completeness. We cannot grasp the infinite. Yet within the limit of our powers we can secure and retain a knowledge which shall be larger than we can bound, and can be thoroughly trustworthy. Our thought of the Absolute Being, for whom God is the accepted and sufficient name, will be more distinct at certain times and in certain persons than in other minds and under different conditions. But the consciousness of his being is fixed in our nature and cannot be removed, nor long suppressed. "The manifestation of the unknowable" is to be found in all things. Then it would seem that so far He is not the unknowable, if we give to words their usual significance. Reality and degree are not identical, and we know in part. "The belief in a Power of which no limit in Time or Space can be conceived is that fundamental element in Religion which survives all its changes of form." "This inexpugnable consciousness, in which Religion and Philosophy are at one with Common-Sense, proved to be likewise that on which all exact Science is based." The "necessary datum of consciousness" sustains the confident appeal which is made to it. I have repeated the word and thought of Spencer. He did not approve the conclusion of Mansel, which he quotes; yet in view of all which has just been said, while confessing the limits of intelligence and of obligation, in our ordinary manner of thinking and speaking it does not seem too much to assert, that "It is our duty to think of God as personal; and it is our duty to believe that He is infinite."

The belief in powers greater than man, in nature or beyond it, though often dim and rude, hardly to be discerned, is apparently nowhere entirely wanting. The universal and persistent instincts which stand in our creation are with authority. The religions of the world, various as the tribes of men, confess a divine presence. The Greek saw a Father in Zeus, whom he addressed as Father of gods and men. Upon Mars' Hill St. Paul appealed to the Athenians whose city was crowded with altars, and declared the unknown God who made the world and all things therein, in whom we live and move and have our being, and confirmed his teaching by their own poet, Aratus:

> With Zeus begin we. Let no mortal voice
> Leave Zeus unpraised. Zeus fills the haunts of men,
> The streets, the marts. Zeus fills the sea, the shores,
> The harbours, — everywhere we live in Zeus.
> We are his offspring too.
> Men worship Him, the First, the Last.
> Their Father — Wonderful — their Help and Shield.

They were "somewhat superstitious," the courteous preacher remarked; but from their superstition he attempted to lead them in rational ways to God. The argument for his being which is found in marks of design can never lose its force. The common mind will trace the signs of thought and plan, and cannot be persuaded from it. It will find "a permanent guiding influence." The eye is the witness to the design which was in its making, and the star whose light it catches; the lily, and the child's fingers closing around it.

When Vanini, burned as an atheist, was asked if he believed in God he took a straw from the floor and made it his answer. Not convincing, possibly; but after this method men will reason to the end. The habit leagues itself with the native feeling of the soul, and looks up to God. It takes a finer form, and the love of nature which distinguished the Aryan people rises till it finds the answering love beyond. But who shall measure "the Great Necessity"? Asa Gray saw the presence of design in the "exquisite adaptations" in which he delighted; and he believed that "without the implication of a superintending wisdom nothing is made out, and nothing credible." He liked to watch the changing forms of life as it was led along "beneficial lines." His innocent, "indefatigable hours" were rich in the thought of the God whom he loved.

It is an impressive moment when a man feels himself in the presence of his Creator. The deeps of his nature are moved. All that is divine responds to the divine life which touches, encloses, arouses it. Such moments are not very rare. In some degree they are even common. They might be more common and to our great advantage. I call to mind as I say this one whose popular fame among us began with his "Lectures on the Plan of the Creation." His voice hesitating with a strange language, his hand skilful to draw what he could not tell, his new learning, his magnificent countenance, carried him quickly into his deserved and sustained renown. Yet there were few times in his long life when the man was seen so grandly as on the day when he opened his summer school at Penikese. The island barn had been made ready, the swallows whose nests were undisturbed flew in and out, the breeze from the sea came pleasantly through the open doors, the scholars who had gathered for the rare privilege of learning from him waited for his voice. He was not the teacher, not yet; the peace, the light, the young life, the surrounding waters, the outlying world and worlds, appealed to his sensitive heart, and he could not teach. He could only pray, and bid the rest pray with him. Into the light, into the spirit which was closer than the air, to the Creator among whose works they stood, silently he breathed out his prayer. He had not thought to do so, probably; he felt the divine presence, and he had to speak to it in adoration, before he spoke to men of its works. Thus life confessed the fellowship of life. He was drawn aside, drawn and impelled. Nothing in all the history of his schools is finer than the sight of that great soul exchanging thought with its Maker. He is renowned in the scientific world for "classification." He classified himself with God.

After that it was little to write that " A physical fact is as sacred as a moral principle." For a physical fact is a moral principle. Whether a divine thought is expressed in stone or statute, in the descent of a glacier or the framing of a law, it witnesses to its origin. " Our own nature demands of us this double allegiance," he said. This double allegiance ruled in the old astronomer, who looked at night from among his sheep into the nearer sky, and sang of the stars and Him who lighted them; " The heavens declare the glory of God." Then he lost sight of the stars, and still he sang, " The law of the Lord is perfect, restoring the soul." His whole being thrilled with the glory and perfection, visible and invisible, till he longed to be in harmony with the beauty around him. " Let the words of my mouth and the meditation of my heart be acceptable in thy sight, O Lord, my rock and my redeemer." Here, again, was the life in a man claiming kinship with the divine life which it felt.

To come nearer, one of the most sublime places on which I have ever stood was the upper bridge of a large steamer in mid-ocean and at night. The ship with her hundreds of souls was quiet beneath, while driven onward by the hidden forces within her. The throb was felt, the power was concealed. Around stretched the sustaining sea, in the dimness unpeopled. Above were the silent heavens, pointed with light, and closer than the world, clearer to the sight than the deck over which the shadows of men flitted. It was, in its feeling, almost to be away from the earth and among the stars. Then the gray-haired officer turned his optic glass to a planet thousands of miles beyond, and caught its light, and learned from it where we were upon the waste of waters. A sailor stood with a lantern that the telltale figures might be registered. There was no sound. Solemnity as of another world rested on the little group of men. To my unaccustomed heart it was more than easy to feel the life which filled the limitless space, to see the fingers which marked their courses for the stars, to be aware of God. For it was life answering to life.

How delightful, how superb, for man to know God, to be assured of his presence; to know himself, also; to be conscious of his life, to feel the fellowship of his breath with the breath from which it was breathed, and the intercourse of soul with soul! I do not know that it is demonstrated.

Perhaps it is better. The best things are rather felt than proved.

The conscience, too, speaks for God. It represents Him in the human soul. It recognizes its sovereign, and declares only its derived authority. All the provinces of the right acknowledge Him. The moral order of the world calls for a moral orderer; a power ruling for righteousness; insuring the good of those who do right, and with judgment visiting the evil-doer. We may find on every side, without, within, the "indelible marks of a morally constituted world, moving toward righteous ends." Kant was reasonable in his argument that in another world the deserts of men, delayed here, must be meted out to them, and that this means God. "For right is right, since God is God." Even beyond the thought of results, of reward or loss, truth and right claim our allegiance. With authority and high sanctions does duty address itself to us and command obedience.

Turn where we will, in the mind of man lies the necessity for God, the Eternal, the Perfect, the Almighty. We like the simple description which Victor Hugo gives of the old woman: "A pious creature, poor, and charitable to the poor and even to the rich, who could just write her name, 'Marguerite,' and believed in God, which is knowledge. There are many such virtues down here, and one day they will be up above, for this life has a morrow."

I am not trying to demonstrate the existence of God, as if to those who do not know it. I am not ignorant of the replies that are spoken after our reasoning. There is sadness in them all. It would be a terrible thing to live in a world without God. It is a fearful thing to live and not see Him. "I will not leave you orphans," the Teacher said. After all replies men still know there is God. It is man who knows it; who feels it in himself, sees it in the world, reads it in history, discerns it in experience, perceives it in the moral order which encloses him, finds it when he sounds his deepest intuitions; the feelings, principles, aspirations, which underlie his life. If to any one it seems too bold a thing to say that man is a necessity, it is not much too bold. For akin to the need for God, if any life is to be, is his need of one to know Him; to receive of his life and love; to braid the thread of divine thought which encompasses him with the thread of human thought which, unbroken, reaches the Eternal. Life must create. It is its nature and pleasure; and creation is the larger name of man. It is a stupendous truth that man knows his Maker and is instructed to call him Father, for that is his Name.

I have spoken the two words which are at the opening of our study — God, Man. In the beginning God, afterward man; and the life of God is the life of man. "The descent into our own souls is the ascent to God." "To penetrate the secret of man is to discover the truth of God." "He hath made everything beautiful in its time; also He hath set eternity in the heart of man."

II

THE COURSE OF MAN IN THE OLDEST LITERATURE

THE COURSE OF MAN IN THE OLDEST LITERATURE

THE new world had its tenant. He was in the image and likeness of the Maker of both house and householder. It was fitting that it should be so, if the world was to fulfil its design, and there was to be agreement through the whole plan and in the method of its working out. Neither man nor world was a mechanism which could run, or was desired to run, by its own force, or after its own skill. The power which had made was the power which was prepared to keep. Between God and the earth was man. By steps which we cannot measure, or describe, he had come to his estate; and to all which made him like the living creatures over whom he had a delegated dominion, and who answered to the names he gave, was added the spiritual endowment in which he was like his Creator. The union of the two kinds of life was exact, but the difference between them was infinite. The words under which so many have passed into the sacred quiet of Mount Auburn remind us in our most thoughtful mood of a separation which was distinct from birth: "Then shall the dust return to the earth as it was; and the spirit shall return unto God who gave it." The part which was "contextured in the Loom of Heaven," as Carlyle describes it, is to be laid aside. But the spirit ascends. "Well said Saint Chrysostom, with his lips of gold, the true Shekinah is Man." In him God's presence is manifested to our eyes and hearts. To tell precisely where the line which divides must be drawn is beyond the wit of man. I think that we prefer to have it so. But man was created in the "image of God." The description is exalted. There is no stop, no pause even, on the way. The likeness reaches the Creator. By no stretch of the imagination could man be said to be in the likeness of anything which had been made. How completely all thought of an origin less than divine is ruled out by such a word as "image"! The greatness of man proclaims the greatness of his Creator. But is the word "image" proper? Evidently it is. If man is not an accident, a chance appearance, the thought which he has fulfilled belonged to one greater than himself. To be able to think man, and to give him being, required God. Man is to be accounted for. No way has been found but this. That man is able to think of God and does think of Him, is suggestive of his origin and descent. Pascal's familiar words are heavy with meaning: "Man is but a reed, the weakest in nature, but he is a thinking reed. Were the universe to crush him, man would still be more noble than that which kills him, because he knows that he dies, and the universe knows nothing of the advantage it has over him." The fathers felt the divine creative presence. They certainly did not worship "an absentee God, sitting idle ever since the first Sabbath, at the outside of his universe." They believed in providence, in a special providence, and felt there was a power around them and beyond them to be worshipped and loved. They lived in his light, died under his shield, looked for his reward. They were "made of the same stuff of which events are made." It is not difficult to trace in man the likeness to his Maker which is his grand distinction. He thinks, reasons, recalls; he has conscience, will, freedom; he can govern and judge himself; he has visions of the future, with aspirations and ambitions which resemble foreknowledge; he feels his endless life. With this he knows his Creator, listens to Him, speaks to Him, obeys Him, loves Him, by virtue of the response of his nature to the life which gave it and maintains it. In a phrase written long afterward, he is a "partaker of the divine nature." In the revised version a psalmist is made to say that man was made "but little lower than God." We prefer the epistle which shows him "a little lower than the angels."

We have not come upon that word until now, for it is not in our present purpose, and I do not know where the angels should enter in. Before man, doubtless, but in the same order of intelligence, for we can hardly think of the vast spaces as uninhabited save by the Eternal, or of his countless years as giving Him no fellowship beyond Himself. There is room for all that we wish to imagine, and imagination has neither neglected nor overstepped its opportunity. What we read of angels enhances the dignity of man as of one esteemed worthy of such ministries as are ascribed to the celestial beings, whose appearance is in dazzling light and gleaming robes, when some rare event calls for their presence. Yet their service is with discrimination.

Ruskin's remarks will be in place here: "You will always find that, in proportion to the earnestness of our own faith, its tendency to accept a spiritual personality increases; and that the most vital and beautiful Christian temper rests joyfully in its conviction of the multitudinous ministry of living angels, infinitely varied in rank and power." Instances of their ministry, as we all know, are frequent in our sacred records, and in the annals of other peoples. They had their part in the one grand purpose which moves in our Scriptures. But it is a significant fact, which carries evidence of the sincerity of the writers of the Gospels, and of the restraint under which they held themselves, that when Christ came angels were at the manger, but that at the end they were not at the Cross. Legions might have been summoned, but not one brightened the darkness by the shining of his wings.

Few truths could be of more service in bringing man to the right apprehension of himself, and of his place in the universe, in quickening a high self-respect and a regard for his splendid possibilities in character and achievement, than that which at once declares and continually asserts his relation to the Eternal. We have grown so accustomed to low views of humanity that our reckoning is at fault. We are like ships that have lost their place and can get no observation by reason of thick clouds and broken instruments. Dead reckoning is a poor reliance. Who is responsible for the inaccurate, dishonoring opinions which prevail concerning man it were of no use to inquire, unless possibly we should be led to see the truth with our own eyes and judge with our own mind and heart. But it is only just to say that the Bible is not to be charged with this misleading, for it labors to persuade men of their greatness, and to induce them to make this actual, to regain their birthright, to lay claim to all which is designed for them. The writers depict men as they find them, and the portrayal is sad; but they do not stop on this. Their design is not to make us aware of our misery, but to bring us out of it. They set forth the beginning and the true end. They deal with the present, but they pronounce this neither the beginning nor the close. They declare it a departure, and reach out a hand to guide men in the right way. They cover reproaches with promises. As at the first, the evening and the morning make the day, and the morning lasts. The Bible has suffered at the hands of those whom it has sought to help, when they have refused to read its teachings through to the closing sentences, with an intelligent thoroughness, but have made selections, according to their inclination and disposition, and have missed its spirit, and the steady trend of its instruction, the glorious uplift of its truths. "O Israel, thou hast destroyed thyself; but in me is thine help. . . . O Israel, return unto the Lord thy God; for thou hast fallen by thine iniquity;" thus the Hebrew prophet summoned his people to their place. Repent, Return, are characteristic words. "Remember from whence thou art fallen, and repent, and do the first works," is one of the latest calls of the New Testament, with the Good News of God. The teaching is not that man's ascent, while real, is too slow, and needs to be aided and hastened; but that there should be a turning, a returning, and then an advance. The word of Christ to the Jewish ruler is as full of hope and promise as of counsel — "Except a man be born anew, he cannot see the kingdom of God." The man saw the meaning of the words, as his answer shows. But the call and promise were renewed and with added force.

It is in the light of these teachings, at once profound and sublime, holding the past and the present in their view, that President James Walker's words find their significance: "The Gospel is a Divine dispensation of encouragement." If any one bases his low estimate of man and his estate upon the Bible, it is because he has not read it. No book which deserves reading can be read by disconnected portions. Sometimes in our impatience with the deliberate movement of a book we take the last pages before their time, to see how things "come out." I think if men had taken this method with the Bible they would have been less offended by the events through which the history moves steadily toward its consummation. I do not say that the last should be read first, but that it should be read. Seeing we have the end, it may be well sometimes to begin there. The final view of man is good enough to satisfy any one. But the line is unbroken from the beginning. One ray of light connects the earth and the sun, and shows us both.

Nor is the depressed and depressing view of man to be so much charged upon the theologians as some have hastily said. They have indeed many times drawn in dismal colors his condition and his destiny. They have at times aroused more fear than hope, which was not Scriptural. But they have not failed to remind men from what a height they have fallen, nor to point out the way of recovery. They have had a high idea of the value of a man, although their views conflicted with their opinions on other subjects. If they have limited expectation under the stress of their philosophy, they have still declared the origin of the race and drawn in weary lines its departure. It may be, and it may not be, strange that readers have missed the better part of their teaching through the offence of the other portions. This has not been fair, but the blame for the impression they have left lies not altogether at the door of the old divines. I am not called to defend them. They belong in their time. They had their work and did it, and exceeded it. They had the approval of strong men. They made strong men, who thought and dared and achieved. The old systems lacked gentleness, but they abounded in vigor. If they were not encouraging, they were robust. We see defects in their philosophy. Let us not overlook the witness which was in them, or their conserving nature, or the special place which was assigned to each in the procession of theologies. What has been said of one of the greatest of the old masters might be said of others: that in their intense desire to exalt God, and to have Him seen in his sovereignty, man was made to appear small. He was nothing, that God might be everything. It is against that conclusion I have been contending. If one makes comparison of man with his Maker, man must of necessity be small and of slight account. We are not called to such a contrast. While, on the other hand, the greater God is, the greater is he who is made in his likeness; and the greater man is, the greater is God who is his Maker, and whose image he bears. Father and child stand in common grandeur, even while the grandeur of the Father is infinite. Indeed, a part of the greatness of a man, a sign of his worth, appears in the unbounded reverence wherewith he stands, kneels, before his Creator.

An attempt has been made by a great preacher to show the "dignity of human nature from its ruins." He finds in pieces of paved road and antique milestones, in broken walls and fallen columns, witness to the greatness of perished cities and empires. So he discovers "the true majesty of human nature itself, in the tragic grandeur of its disorders." In the worst passions, in hopes and fears, in false religions and gropings for light, in spiritual intelligence astray from truth, in the blind, uncertain thought of God, he discerns the marks of a higher estate. This is ingenious and interesting, and has its value. But we reach the same end by a shorter path as we mark the dignity of human nature as shown by its origin. Whatever has come in since, the start was noble. It could not have been better. In the despoiled temple we imagine the Parthenon in its integrity. If we had the plans of the architect, from which it was constructed, and knew his design, we might reach even a higher estimate of its majesty. This advantage we have when we study man. The order of events is the true order of history. In the beginning, God; then man, whose life is the divine breath, and the end toward which creation slowly moved. The summit was reached. The world had come to its meaning. In man the Creator was in affectionate and intelligent connection with the world. It was not to be ruled by power, but governed by love. The response of the world to its Maker is from the heart of man. We do well to appreciate the divine intent. Speaking after our own manner, if God was to keep the world He must keep man. He was the one point at which God, who is spirit, could enter the world's life. If He lost man He lost the earth. It is not self-praise if, standing here, we exclaim, How magnificent is Man! How fine his nature, the thought, the will, the love, the conscience, the choice, the divine life! What may we not look for as the powers of man come into use, grow by exercise, prove themselves in conduct, construct character, reveal the Eternal in whose likeness they have their being!

There is one life; of that life is the life of a man. It is to be kept true to itself; to be in him what it was before he knew it. The higher nature is to rule the life. I give a rough illustration. I fill my cup from the brook by the way. The water is not changed in the transfer. The brook is in the cup. The breath of the Creator is not changed by entering the nostrils of the man, and is not to be changed beyond them.

If we consider who and what man was at the first, it is clear that his business in the world, up to the limit of his powers, was to be like his Maker; to think, choose, live like Him. By being like God he was to preserve himself and justify his appointment as the crown of creation and the head of the world. Surely there is something superb here. With all his ambition and pride and glory, no man has ever esteemed himself highly enough. Many have made wrong estimates, and have been conceited and foolish. But no one has put too great value upon his birthright in having for his daily life the breath of the Eternal. Pride would exalt itself, if it would become rational and ascend into Religion. If there is honest comfort in self-respect, here is its boundless opportunity. Godly, Godlike, is not a word merely, a well-sounding adjective, but the honest expression of all that is becoming in that divine life which is man. It would be truth in the inward parts corresponding to the eternal truth. It would not be imitation, but the natural expression of being. Nothing could be more explicit than the requirement of Christ, which we may well accept as the privilege of the beginning, "Ye therefore shall be perfect, as your heavenly Father is perfect." St. Peter quoted from Leviticus, "Be ye holy, for I am holy." He added that "divine power hath granted unto us all things that pertain unto life and godliness, through the knowledge of Him that called us by his own glory and virtue."

The time has come for another new word. We are advancing in philology. There is a term which is essential to moral character, that is, to manhood. No one would hesitate to say that the man ought to preserve his life in its purity and divinity; ought to keep the divine breath which he has received like the breath of which it was an inseparable part. He cannot improve it; let him preserve it. Even without a commandment, the propriety of this is evident. There is obligation, responsibility; the words grow as we think. As defining the man's relation to himself and to his Maker "ought" is a serious word. It carries a theology in its letters. It is a covenant and a sacrament. In its principles it is as firm as gravitation, or anything which in our poverty we call "law." It is character, it is life. It holds honor and well-being. It is religion. It connects man with the universe and the Creator. When we call conscience "the vice-regent of God" we write "ought" in large letters. We have "the inflashing" upon the conscience of that which we must do, and we assent to this, and meet without complaint the result of our misdoing. This is our original nature. What is the ground of this authority over us? It has been said to be in our creation. We do not feel this, for our making was not of our desire. Nor do we feel that strength gives the right to rule, nor does experience of results content us. We get farther back into the nature of the Creator. He is perfect. To be like Him is to be perfect. We know that the best should be enthroned, and that our allegiance should be given to it. This reason declares, and conscience, and nature. Here we have the best in stability and strength. Say "God is love," and no more is to be desired. To require the man to be like his Maker is to ask him to be his best, the best man he can be. "Our chief want in life is somebody who shall make us do what we can," the philosopher said. Duty is that friend; unobtrusive to the willing, but unswerving as the poles.

There is often a comfort in this fact. When we are bewildered among questions of conduct, we come back to this with assurance. Here the ground is solid. It is a strong passage in the life of the soldierly English preacher, Frederick Robertson, when there came to him accumulated trouble — the ruin of a friendship, the breaking of his health, deep darkness which buried the light in his soul — and his early faiths were shattered; one truth remained and to that he clung, and with it fought his way to safety. It was this, "It must be right to do right." Good! But what is it to do right? What is right? "Be true," he said, "be true." True to what? The eternal answer is in the beginning, is here, is everywhere, is forever. Be yourself; and yourself is of God's self. Be like Him. Think, desire, will, with Him. "Thy will be done." Religion needs this vigor of right conduct; to be robust in virtue. The point is well made, that religion is not morality touched by emotion, but emotion touched by morality. If the life were obedience, it would be in liberty, for there is no other obedience. It would be glad, for it is the thought of the eternal gladness, and as natural as the fragrance of flowers, the song of birds. I do not know that this had any name at first. In the time of Moses, when conduct had taken on more form it was called Love, and no better name was found when Christ defined it. He connected this with life when He bade his disciples, "If ye love me keep my commandments." It was in all its course delight, blessedness responding to blessedness, in a rivalry of pleasing. This was at the first. It seems to have continued. It is one of the universal traditions, that the first dwellers upon the earth knew an " Edenic happiness," which means truth, rightness, obedience. "This belief in an age of happiness and of innocence in the infancy of mankind may be found among all peoples of the Aryan and Japhetic race;" and "this is one of the points where their traditions find themselves most evidently on common ground with the Semitic stories which we find in Genesis." The Egyptians had their golden age to which they continually looked back. It was the time of Ra, "who inaugurated the existence of the world and of human life," and who ruled the earth. To assert the superiority of anything above all that could be imagined, it was sufficient to say that "its like had never been seen since the days of the god Ra." We move on; but I cannot attempt to describe the various views of the students of man and his history. There is no need of doing it here, nor does it concern my design.

Man is presented by one school as "the crown and glory of the universe and the chief object of divine care, yet still the lame and halting creature, loaded with a brute-inheritance of original sin, whose ultimate salvation is slowly to be achieved through ages of moral discipline." But sin and salvation are here diverted from the usual and natural meaning of the terms; yet even thus there is "a struggle between his lower and his higher impulses, in which the higher must finally conquer;" and there is claimed to be in this "the strongest imaginable incentive to right living." Or, again, we are told that "man rises out of the animal stage and becomes a man," and thus comes under the law of God, "the law of right and wrong."

It is of importance to mark that the idea of the right, of duty, of the ought, holds its place in this method of regarding life. The persistence of that truth is to be always in mind. What I have to insist upon is this, as a part of the larger truth, that in some way, at some time, "man became a living soul," a soul like the divine life, and that in the course of time there was one walking the earth who had the faculty we name "Conscience," which binds a man to his Maker in a common nature, with a community of purpose and conduct. There was a person who ought. Infinite and finite are words easily spoken; but let us not fail to notice that, with all the distance between them, they are in the same line.

We are brought now to the real and vital question: what, under the conditions of his life, this person would do. In some way man came to be man. Let all the time which is thought necessary be taken for this. It is certainly not unreasonable, but to be expected, that this coming of age should be attended and followed by a time of true manhood, upright, honest, godly; and that unbroken happiness should prevail. What followed does not make this irrational. From the time when man found himself he may well have lived in gladness until the time when he lost himself. That he pushed down, or pushed up, into another estate is clear. But he may have paused on the way from an innocent animal to whatever came afterward, and paused long enough to enjoy the rest. From this he may have made a new start.

I am well aware that this view is not in accord with the independent opinions which are cherished by many students; that they see no space for paradise with a true and righteous manhood; no pause in life into which it could have been set. The emergence from a lower condition is constant, and constantly forward. By slow degrees man acquired higher qualities, and ascended to his true estate. There is no reason why this doctrine of ascent should not include the happy condition which the traditional literature we possess clearly describes. The weight cast into the scales of opinion by a few pages of unknown origin may not be great, but it would seem to be heavy enough to move the beam which is held by an impartial, uncommitted hand. If we are left to inference, certainty is impossible.

Man was not alone in the world. He touched life on every side. It is not easy to define his relation to it in definite terms. The alliance of man with the life around him and beneath him is delicate and mysterious. It is real; but the process of advance from it is not perfectly clear. Much of our reasoning seems to do discredit to the less endowed creatures, to depreciate the inferior life by comparison. It is true that what is proper in them may be wrong in a man. Yet they live out their best nature. If man had done so, the story of the world had been very different.

In this connection it is impressive, instructive, to observe the care of God for the humbler creatures whom He had made, and their recognition of his goodness. Classical literature knew nothing of this, but in the Hebrew Bible it has its place. The Hebrews were a people of less culture and taste than the Greeks, but they had a fuller idea of God. Their account of the attendant providence is far in advance of the other descriptions. Let me read a verse or two from an unknown Hebrew writer: "The young lions seek their meat from God. These all wait upon Thee, that Thou mayest give them their meat in due season. Thou openest thine hand, they are satisfied with good." It would be difficult to match this thought in the poets of other nations. When we attempt to adjust our relations with these companions in other orders of life they are at a disadvantage which is insuperable, in that they cannot speak for themselves. If only our poor relations could tell their thoughts! Who looks into the eyes of a fine dog, down into the deeps of his life, and does not pity him that he cannot speak? Perhaps it was meant that our fellowship upon that side should not be very close, lest we forget whose children we are. But we do not smile at the poor Indian's thought of the continued companionship he shall have in "that equal sky."

There is something natural, kindly, helpful, in the friendship of man with his less favored kindred. I do not know that this can be taught or learned. It seems to be nature's assertion of itself: life reaching down somewhat as it reaches up. Kinship makes itself felt. I can readily imagine the delight of St. Francis of Assisi in preaching to birds. " My little sisters, the birds," he said, and he bade them praise their Creator who had given them liberty to fly about everywhere; and had given them the air to live in, and had fed and clothed them, and preserved them in the ark. The birds listened, bowing their heads and spreading their wings, and by their songs showing that the Father had given them joy exceeding great.

He spoke and they sang. It were a pity to ask if they knew what he said, and answered it. They had life in common with him. They were "the clothed form" and spirit of the air. Their presence found him and his presence moved them. They enjoyed this, and it was pleasant to him. Let us leave something for imagination and fancy. The preaching, at least, was real; whether it was heard and heeded is another matter. But it is pertinent to say, that if the hearing and responding are essential to preaching, much which goes by that name has a questionable title to it.

We are learning to be more than kind to those who are more than faithful; yet one holds his friend "better than his dog" and "dearer than his horse." I believe that the form next below us has not yet been found. If he were I do not think we should care for him. He would be "so near and yet so far" that we should prefer our dog. I think it is well that we have never made his acquaintance. We are not detained here. Nearly all the voices bid us go on, — hope, aspiration, ambition, religion, — and life itself. After all, "our citizenship is in heaven."

The difference of opinion in regard to other

things is not essential to the purpose we have now in hand. We have more important questions.

Would man, when he had been made a man, consent to be godly; to live as God did, by the will of God? Of ability there was no lack. That was essential to manhood. The divine breath, which was the soul's life, held that unchanged. It was a matter of will, of choice, in the use of liberty. Let us not be confused by differing views of his history up to this place. He came to this estate. Whatever else was true, there he was, at the point where he was to make up his conduct. He was free, or it would have been trifling to describe him as in the image of God. It was not a liberty in which he might choose what should be right. That was utterly out of his reach. As well choose the time when the sun should rise, or the tide come in. His divine nature, before it was his own, had determined the right. Richard Hooker's words, often repeated, carry no marks of time: "Law has her seat in the bosom of God; her voice is the harmony of the world." Mr. Emerson taught that the weight of the universe presses down upon the shoulders of every moral being to hold him to his place. It is a heavy load, but there is no escape from it. We make it easy by keeping at our post cheerfully, and standing erect, holding the universe. Atlas can bear the world if he stands straight. The liberty resided in the power to say whether he would do that which he ought, or would disown it, and do — something else. That for a time he chose to do the right is probable. How far this continued we have not been told; we have not a tradition, even. Documentary evidence is scant, but what we have is easily read. Can it be trusted? The ancient writing has been so well confirmed, as far as we can trace elsewhere the occurrences which it describes, that it seems irrational to leave it here. Up to this point the results of later studies are in remarkable agreement with it, as we have seen. Why should the tradition, if it is that, suddenly fail us? We have the two records, but the parts have one editor. These writings are certainly convenient in their simple narrative and cannot be lightly esteemed. In referring to the early chapters of the Bible, I made use of them as a statement of events with which science has to do. I now use them as a statement of events with which history has to do. They are useful for this purpose, and have at least the authority which belongs to early literature, confirmed so far as it may be from other sources. The literary, or scientific, presumption is that having been true up to this point they continue to be true.

The transition from man obedient and happy to man wrong and ashamed is very abrupt in the Hebrew story. Longer time may have been taken than the brief narrative suggests. We are reading of the innocent delight of the man and woman in their safe and beautiful life, when, without warning, we come upon this: "Now the serpent." The writer goes on to tell of a change; of the time when man chose not to be like God, when his life swerved and went its own way. He is soon discovered in this estate, at variance with the divine nature which has been given him. Now I stand beside the brook and look into the cup, and the water in the cup is not like the water in the brook. Of this, unhappily, no proof is required. The daily papers keep it before our eyes. The voluminous histories of all times force it upon our notice. It is in drama and poetry; in law and legislation. We see it wherever we turn, and feel it within us, and trace it as far as history runs. No man who knows God can think He made the world of men to be what it is. The gift of liberty, essential to manhood, has been found a perilous endowment. Account for it as we may, here are the facts: explanations are of less consequence.

Who does not observe the change from the first days — a change in human thought since the life of the Eternal became the life of man? Let it not be forgotten that many regard the evil of history and experience as belonging in the lower life from which man has imperfectly escaped; — "Very imperfectly," an observer would remark, — that he is thought to have risen greatly and to be slowly ascending. Give him time, and of this there is enough, — what need to be parsimonious when we have centuries at our command, — give him the ages, and he will be a credit to himself and them. This is an explanation seriously made, and it is to be seriously regarded. In this view the divine life was of such a nature, and was given by such degrees, that it was not able quickly to overrule the lower life to which it was joined. This would reduce obligation to an inconsiderable force. The result, instead of being a defect, would be an approach toward an increasing victory, and from this much might be hoped. I have no occasion to discuss this, for I am concerned with man after he has reached the stage of moral life, or obligation. I see the advance of man and his improvement in many ways, material, intellectual, social, and perhaps moral. But I cannot make the long course of the world, as it is working by the natural forces within it, a movement toward the Creator, and the recognition of itself as his world. I do not see that man untaught is finding himself as the child of God, whose spirit is divine, and wills to be divine; who is governed, sustained, comforted, by "the power of an endless life." If man of his own nature is on his way to a divine life, the road is terribly long. And, oh, the pain and sorrow and cruelty and dying all the way, from a time no one has discovered! It seems like Napoleon's retreat from Russia, infinitely extended.

> Are God and Nature then at strife,
>   That Nature lends such evil dreams?
>   So careful of the type she seems,
> So careless of the single life.

It is very well to say that in some other world man will attain to himself. That is poor comfort. Is this good world to go for nothing? Are countless generations to suffer, that thousands of years hence there may be one wherein a man knows who he is, and begins to live as a man ought to live? I don't believe it. It seems to me not like God, and not like man. Improvement, progress, development, — I grant them all. But this is man himself; whose interests are as real now as they ever will be; for whom to-day should have its full value as truly as any coming day; for whom the right is as right as it will be æons hence; to whom ought has its full significance, even to the possibility, and, alas! the reality, of the wrong. But let me interpose the thought, and ask special attention to it, that even if the steady improvement of man is provided for, and will go on unto perfection, there is nothing to prevent the Creator and Father from assisting, hastening, securing, the movement in any way which He chooses. He may do this by a new and special bestowment of spiritual life; or by great men, prophets, and the like; or in the Son of Man. Indeed, seeing how much is involved, both for Himself and for the world, the natural advance is so deliberate as to be almost a promise of added help.

The Hebrew description is in accord with all that we know of the conditions, and in agreement with history and constant observation, as it has reached us in a few simple sentences out of the shadowy past in which some facts stand up like mountain peaks. There came a time, whatever preceded it, when man was to choose whether he would live according to the higher nature which was his; that is, according to the will of the Creator whose life was his; or live in another way, after other desires. The thought came to him, was given to him, — to the woman who had joined him, and then to the man, — of a new knowledge, wherein they should be as God. They were to be like God by becoming unlike Him. It is all foolish, of course. Sin is always foolish. But the new desire prevailed. This has been termed "The Fall." I do not remember that the Bible uses that word in describing the event. Some one called it "a fall up." But "a fall up" is a fall down. The idea that this was merely a step in ethical growth is queer, or seems so.

It is hard to be rid of our questioning, which returns upon us: When did man come to the place where he began to live? Or has he reached it yet? There is no ethical life till man can choose for himself what he will do. Has he not yet reached that point? What becomes of Abraham if we are still fiercely and with slender hopes struggling with our brute inheritance, and if this explains our wars and fightings and envyings and confusions! No. The old account is the best we have, short as it is. Let the lower nature of man be granted. Already he knows his higher nature, and he knew it in the garden we call Eden. The story is very brief, but is like the annals of which it is a part. Regarded as history, parable, allegory, picture, there it is, and it is consistent in its whole extent. It is a simple world which is presented, and simple lives are lived upon it. The narrative of the second chapter is properly connected with the first. A garden describes in pleasant form the abode of men, and keeping it was their occupation. The life around them was fearless and friendly.

> About them frisking play'd
> All beasts of th' earth, since wild.

Days were not wearisome in their healthful employment, and nights were the repose of innocence. The joy of life was theirs, and

> In their looks divine
> The image of their glorious Maker shone.

The commandment which stated their duty is in the language of the garden: "Of the tree of the knowledge of good and evil, thou shalt not eat of it." The meaning and design were plain to those to whom the words were spoken. We have in the narrative an illustrated account of things as they were. There is a philosophy in the imagery which has contented very sensible men. These were the conditions, so far as they have been disclosed, under which the departure began, and the departing took its form from them. It is well to mark the simplicity here in comparison with all other accounts of this part of human experience: "When the woman saw that the tree was good for food, and that it was a delight to the eyes, and that the tree was to be desired to make one wise, she took of the fruit thereof and did eat; and she gave also unto her husband with her, and he did eat." Thus the will of God and the will of man were opposed. The life of man departed from the life of God in desire and deed, in motive and direction. These words, and this representation, once had meaning, and they have meaning still. They bear signs of the primitive times in which they first had their place. The truth which the simple picture was designed to preserve and to transmit has not been outgrown and set aside. I have no occasion now to read these compact sentences as the theologian must. They did eat of forbidden fruit. The fact is all which is here of concern to us, and that remains whatever construction is given to the words. The symbolism also remains, however it may be translated. If we do not like the terms "tree" and "fruit," we are at liberty to make any substitution which scholarship permits. There is no reason why we should be offended or bewildered. The narrative in all its pictorial, representative, symbolic character is harmonious throughout. There is no confusion in the rhetoric or its images. The garden is natural in the story of creation. The garden readily suggests the trees. How should we describe this in a poem? We should not put the man and woman in a palace, or on a ship, or make the testing question one of money or office. The garden is the right place for a home and for the proving of life. The serpent offends us most, but he is often in a garden, and he is in his place in this picture. He has a considerable place in the religious symbolism of the ancients. Sometimes he stands for that which is helpful; but in all mythologies he personifies "the nocturnal, hostile power, the evil principle, material darkness, moral wickedness." The question of the Indian concerning the delay of his destruction waits for an answer. It is evident that whatever the serpent stood for has not been killed. In the Apocalypse we read of "the old serpent which is the devil and Satan." There are many things in the history of the world which are like the things the devil would do, if there were a devil. Perhaps there is; or whose footprints are these all over the world? He appears in the New Testament with the same characteristics which are found here. We do not like him. We do not like any part of the events in which he moves. But the whole story would be harmless if we could undo the facts it expresses. We can tear it from our Bibles, but only the volume would be changed, the paper and binding. We cannot undo the long history which takes us back to that place, or to one no better, unless we boldly deny that man's true life began in the image and likeness of his Maker, or at least attained to it and then began.

I do not claim to be impartial. The habit of a lifetime forbids that. But may I say again, that reading as fairly as I can, reading the narrative as it was meant to be read, I have seen no record of this departure which is more to be esteemed than this, for its reasonableness, and the comfort and courage which come with it? The accounts are all very hard reading. Explain as we may, they are very hard reading.

The narratives which have their place in our Bible and its teaching, as we have seen, present to us two persons who have come to the estate of man and woman, who are well grown up, and mature enough to be put in charge of the newly made earth, to have dominion over every living thing that moves upon the earth, or in the sea and air. The man is wise enough to be trusted to give names to all which lives about him. He is mature enough, well-endowed enough, to receive the commandment of God. He stands well in all the first portion of his history. There is a royal character which shows his origin. He is not born of earth. He moves like a god. There comes a change and he moves unlike a god. What God wills he wills not. By some road he comes to the parting of the ways, and he departs from the way of God. It is fearfully sad. A man has been ridiculed for weeping because he sinned in Adam; yet one might be pardoned a tear as the fairness of Eden fades away; fades into the common light.

But why did they — the man and woman of the world — why did they, and thus readily, become false to themselves and their only friend, their Creator, in whose hand their life was, whose life was their life? There has never come any one to tell us. They could do it, or they would not have done it. But to have been unable to do it would have deprived their obedience of its worthiest quality, the freeness of it. An automatic virtue would have been the virtue of trees and birds, extended a little way. I believe it was Huxley who said he should be willing to be wound up every morning like a clock, if it would insure his going right all day. I should not. We would almost prefer to do wrong now and then rather than never do right. Liberty was a genuine gift and held the hazard. Manhood required liberty. In its freedom the will finds what has well been termed "its inalienable prerogative." The assertion of liberty and the appeal to it pervade our Scriptures. Indeed, the Bible would scarcely be necessary without it. "Come unto me," " Ye will not come unto me," are repeated in a thousand forms. To explain this use of the liberty by the stress of temptation is but to throw the unresolved mystery farther back. The fall of angels is even harder to account for than the fall of man. Moral evil was created out of nothing. Goodness could not evolve it, for there was no germ to be developed. Man made it for himself, as it had been made before. It was the act of the will which needs no material. The modern explanation is reasonable, and it suits itself to the picture of the elder time: that man had two natures, that which allied him with the earth and the life upon it, and that wherein he was the child of God. The lower nature warred against the higher, and prevailed. It was not properly his animal nature, as some imply; for the thought was of his mind, and concerned a new knowledge, which was attractive. Plato accounted for it in this way: " The divine portion within them became extinct through admixture of the mortal nature. Then they began to exhibit unbecoming conduct." The Hebrew account is more graphic. It is a translation, and we can make our own. The desire for the fruit and that which belonged with it, knowledge and power, overcame the commandment, and the authority of conscience. Strange? There are things we do not understand; but the man is peculiar who does not know a conflict like that. St. Paul knew it. Has the battle always gone in the same way? Which way? Experience gives most men reason to believe that they are born of some one like Adam.

Let us read the story a little farther. There is some relief in the thought that in the instance before us the suggestion of wrong came from without. They were guileless, those children of the garden, untaught, unlearned in evil, unsuspicious, and they had never heard a lie. They did not know that one could lie, and seek to thwart the will of the eternal goodness. In the childish habit of believing, they believed. It is a sign of immaturity, but things well-nigh as strange have happened since. We have been too often surprised to be utterly and permanently staggered by the first evil choice. Experience might now fairly be expected to stand in the place of innocence for the routing of temptation. Does it? The result was in keeping with the deed and its conditions. Shame and fear, and the dread of the one friendly presence, came at once. The garden had lost its delight. There is not much left to part with when one has lost himself. They had gone through the gate into the strange outer world. Driven out, the record says. But they were out. " The mind is its own place." More than a flaming sword turning every way kept the way of the tree of life. Yet it is of profound interest to find that they had not lost their confidence in the One they had wronged. Out of the garden, when the mother had in her arms the first-born of woman, the mother-heart in joy held up the child, while she let her thought ascend to God, and her voice raise the song of thanksgiving, the oldest psalm preserved to us, "I have gotten a man from the Lord." Are not these the first rude notes of the hymn sung afterward in Judah: "My soul doth magnify the Lord, and my spirit hath rejoiced in God my Saviour. For he hath looked upon the low estate of his handmaiden"? There is something grand in the first Magnificat. It is a prelude to the second. It is beautiful to mark the penitence and faith and joy of the first mother as these are preserved in a few lines. Her heart is still with God, and his goodness she confesses. It is apparent that she tried to bring up her two boys in the fear of the Lord. One resisted her influence and rejected her teaching; but the other believed her and obeyed the voice of God. In him was promise of better things. But he died! Died at his altar. The return was not then.

I am grateful that I am not asked to explain the terms of this ancient chronicle, to distinguish what is the literal fact and what the form in which it appears. I cannot think that any man is able to do this perfectly. There was a new start, less assuring than the first. There are few clear pages in the later history. Whatever was meant by death, it has come in. Not that men were to live always, and in this method of life; but we must believe that the change which advanced them to other worlds would have had no sadness. Why should it? "The gloom, the knell, the pall, the bier," would not have belonged with it. These have come, and all they signify; and the beginning was so fine! What might have been! But why think of that, unless even yet it may be gained?

There are other accounts of these things, as has been said. But they have not gained a place among us. There has been no reason why they should. Yet they are worth reading, if only for the sake of contrast.

The Aryan nations had a conception of their own, of four successive ages of the world. Created things, including man, were to last through twelve thousand divine years, each one of them comprising three hundred and sixty of the years of man. The ages were to be marked by a gradual degeneracy which could be expressed in the names of the metals — gold, silver, brass, and iron. "Our present human condition is the age of iron, the worst of all, even though it did begin with the heroes." It was in India that this scheme was most fully worked out. Among the Parsees there is a different account. They had the twelve thousand years in four equal periods. They gave a natural and weighty emphasis to the distinction between the light and the dark, which passed easily into the distinction between good and evil, where it is still found convenient and expressive. Ormuzd, Ahura Mazda, the highest divinity, was the creator of the good, and dwelt in the perfect light. Ahriman, Angra Mainyus, created an evil universe, and had his seat in the deepest darkness. The two opposing powers were thus apart, with an empty and neutral space between them. Into this intervening space the earth was lowered when Ormuzd had made it, and there it hung "as a kind of outpost." Ahriman saw what was done, and was roused to action. He bored a hole through the earth, and came out upon its surface, where he destroyed the two inhabitants, as he did those who were set in their place. Thus the earth became the field of contest between good and evil. It is impossible to tell with any approach to certainty when or in what place the great prophet and leader of this faith was born, Zoroaster, otherwise Zarathustra, who was valiant against the forces of evil, and worked toward the final triumph of the good. For "at last the powers of good will win the victory by the aid of

Saoshyans, the deliverer who is to come." Then "Ormuzd will gather the whole human race into the eternal light where he dwells." Thus the Parsees, burning the sacred fire, and reverencing the Avesta, their most sacred book, lived in the presence of unseen forces, paying homage to many divinities, to things in heaven and things on the earth, believing in practical goodness, expecting the judgment of molten metal, and waiting for immortality. To describe all their belief in detail would be impracticable here, if it were not impossible. Nor does the modern occidental mind receive much light from their explanation of the mysteries before us, while it reads them with respectful interest. In this matter of the departure of man from God, to which all history bears witness, the accounts are more elaborate, but not more satisfying. That Ahriman was stronger than men is no help to us. How came he to be stronger? How came he to be at all? Evil is pushed one degree farther back, and from the serpent is found in the god. But the relentless "Why?" has no answer.

One thing, never to be lost sight of, which marks the account in Genesis in lines which cannot be effaced, to which our whole moral sense, our religious intuition, our profoundest convictions, assent; before which Conscience stands, throwing its entire force into approbation and admiration, is this — that evil did not begin with God; did not and could not. It came in rebellion against his commandment, in revolt against his will, in defiance of his penalty. To the credit of the account which bears no name, and in its pictures commits itself to our intelligence, let this be borne in mind. All our ideas are confused, and our deepest sentiments are put to rout, unless the Eternal is one and good. When all is said, do we not return with satisfaction to the condensed statements in Genesis, aware of the unfolding which is needed at every point, seeing room for theories and explanations, and willing to have them arise in many forms? Are we not content with the conclusion of an old writer: "Behold, this only have I found, that God made man upright; but they have sought out many inventions"? I have not forgotten that all these things were long ago, and I have assumed our relation to them. We were brought up in that way. Was not the shorter Catechism — shorter, but quite long enough — pronounced in regard to it? I do not mean that we can join our family line to the first man who ever was. Yet we must be descended from him, or from some first man, or first men, who received of the life of his Maker. I see no reason for disturbing the common belief. The condition of things around us and behind us began somewhere. We have seen a rational beginning, and it is easy to trace our relationship. I shall not try to bridge the centuries. Theologians are not agreed about much except the piers. From a small beginning has come a great family, many families, with a common nature which is of greater moment than all which separates us into tribes and nations.

I see no advantage in making excursions into unknown lands. It will be found that the religious history which opens with these unadorned pages is in sad agreement with them in all its lengthened course. Perhaps we shall be more reconciled to the beginning when we approach the end. Men increased. They scattered; when, we cannot tell. They went their ways, and long afterward are found in different places, and with many differences of condition, but in thought and life separate from themselves and from God. Wherever they are seen they have a religion, that is, a belief in powers beyond themselves and mightier than they. It is plain that religion is a part of the common nature. In many other things the separated peoples are unlike, but Plutarch's statement was true in his time, and if we give it a wide meaning remains true: "A city without a temple or an altar, or some order of worship, no man ever saw." There is something in the man which demands a religion and finds it or makes it. Centuries pass, but the need remains and bears witness to the reason which is in it. We cannot mistake the meaning of this flowing on of human thought. It calls to mind the reasoning with which Nansen encouraged himself when his theories were at fault and his way through the ice was undiscovered. He had studied it all out in advance. He expected to find a shallow polar sea and a current which would easily move him upon it. He came to the polar sea and there was no line on board the "Fram" long enough to sound the waters troubled by his daring. His theory of the current was not sustained. He recalled the experience of an older voyager, that Columbus discovered America by means of a mistake made by another, and then he wrote: "Heaven only knows where my mistake will lead us. Only I repeat once more, 'The Siberian driftwood on the coast of Greenland cannot lie, and the way it went we must go.'"

I am not called upon to define the varying religions which the world has known. The study is most interesting; it has drawn many students to itself, and the results of their study are in our hands. With all this instruction we can answer the inquiry which arises at this point, an inquiry of intense significance in view of the untold millions over whom these religions hold sway: What light, what help, do they offer to bring men back to themselves, and to God, their Maker? Out of the confusion comes no answer to create a certain hope.

The problem is this: Man was like God. Man is unlike God. Can he again be like God? Whether men have come up to this place, or have come down to this place, here they are. Can they attain to the fulness of life? Lest our progress should in any way be hindered by this concise statement, let us regard man as now without a proper likeness to his Creator, whatever be the history of the divergence, and inquire if there is a way in which he can become, or can be made, like God. If there are forces working within him to this end, can these be enlarged, quickened, and guided by a new divine force? Is this new force to be found? That there is truth in the world's religions, and that there have been devout souls, more than the few whose names are preserved, who have found their way back, and have made for themselves lives of virtue and beauty and piety, every one should be ready to admit, and with gratitude. But is the way of return open to all people, and what is the help which seeks them and finds them, and what is the highway up to the approval of God? After all our reading we are checked with the question on our lips. The answer would not come to us very readily in any case. It is by no means easy to understand the religion of our neighbor when it differs from our own. To clearly comprehend the religion of another nation, parted from us as the East is from the West, with a method, and expression, and experience, and a habit of mind and heart, quite unlike our own inheritance, and fashioning themselves in forms which to us are strange and confusing and unattractive, is an improbable attainment, if it be not quite out of our reach. Let all this and more be conceded. Still, a way of life which is to serve a nation should be discernible even to Gentiles. Certainly, if it is pointed out to us, we should be able to see it. If its Gospel is translated into our own tongue, its precepts, if not its mysteries, should be disclosed. That a system of recovery which suits and serves the Oriental does not commend itself to us, in this cooler clime, is not of much account. Is there a system which serves him, creates hope, quickens and rewards desire, secures the rising and advance of life, delivers it from bondage, fosters the spiritual nature which is his birthright, as it is ours, and all men's, brings him into the peace of his own conscience, and changes his fear of God into love? This is the real inquiry, and where shall we look for an answer? Anywhere, for all the world is open before us, and men are religious everywhere. We cannot range the earth at once. But we cannot hastily pass by the thoughts of men whose nature and need are as our own, and who have felt the desires which we know so well. No one can enter into the life of the world, into the things which are concerned with life and destiny, without being profoundly impressed, confused and saddened. "Then Job answered and said, Of a truth I know that it is so; but how can man be just with God?" There is no land where the question has not stayed; often, most often, in a poor, blind, broken, fearful shape. The question is a part of the common nature, and there should be an intelligent answer. Is there? Where is it? If we reply, "It is here," here is but a narrow canton of the world. Is it elsewhere? The history of that instructive question, and of the replies which men have fashioned, is not easily read. The scroll which holds it is wrinkled and torn, and the writing is not always legible.

In such studies as are suggested by these brief considerations we soon find that, as in the records of the rocks, there are wide spaces to be filled. We have the beginning, of which we are assured, and then comes a break in the story, while there must have been continuity in the life. Quite naturally the mind turns to India, where the people are very religious and nearly all the chief religions have had a field, and an opportunity to manifest their power and defend their authority. It is impressive that while so much has taken place there, political and religious, India is a land almost without a history. We are ready to send out the wealth of the Indies, that we may bring home the wealth of the Indies, as we are required to do. But the ships do not come back with Plimsoll's line against the water. It is by no light expenditure, and through no simple process, that we can secure what the land of the Ganges has to offer us of faith and thought. We soon leave dates behind us, for they are modern. In that land of mystery everything seems old. Unfortunately things are not old enough. The time of Brahma, the creator, the supreme intelligence dwelling in deep contemplation, is far away, but not so far that we can read a simple story of his life. His work was soon completed, and Vishnu and Siva, his allies, then received the greater honor. The preserver and the destroyer were worshipped, with a multitude of divinities of many sorts. There was small promise of help for the world. Under this teaching sacrifices have abounded, but they have been offered in weariness of the world, where time and the things of time have ceased to be of interest, and in the presence of illusion. Even in this dreariness the people could not stand together, dividing the burden of their dismay, and sharing whatever of good any one chanced to realize, but they separated themselves into the rigid castes which have remained in their power to hinder and oppress.

There was need of a reformer, and he came. It was in the latter half of the sixth century before Christ that Siddhartha, the prince, who came to be known as Buddha, or the Buddha, was born. He early felt the miseries of life and fled from them, and devoted himself to the deliverance of mankind. He found no content in the teachings of the Brahmans. He practised austerities, but they brought him no rest. At length, after a prolonged meditation, he learned the way of rescue which he had sought. Then he went forth to preach, and he made many disciples, and when he died, eighty years old, Buddhism was an established rule of life, which in time extended over India and beyond, and it is said bore sway over a third of the people of the earth. Buddha, the illumined one, who saw and knew the truth, gave to men a person whom they could admire, whose teachings were more definite than they had known, whose spirit and life drew the credence of needy hearts. There is a lasting charm in the story of this life which has kept it familiar. It is not strange that he holds his place among his followers as "the chiefest among ten thousand." In view of all things it is, perhaps, not strange that so large a part of the world should call itself after his name. What better name had they? He could not be shielded from the sight of evil. It was at the door of his house and waited beside his path. He looked beyond and saw evil and misfortune extended in endless returnings. If he could break up the clinging to life he would set men free. If he could teach men the emptiness of all earthly things, and induce them to renounce that in which they found delight, their deliverance would be accomplished. Into what they were to escape he did not make clear. Nirvana has commonly been regarded as the final end of living, though it may not be this. Still, a change so complete as it promised would be the end of such life as men had known upon the earth. In many discourses he taught his doctrine and offered his help. He made great account of man, differing in this from the teachers whom he displaced, who made God everything. He set his mind on time, when the Brahman aspired to eternity. By acts of faith, and obedience, and charity he would bring men into a better estate. The result was, again, disappointing. Unquestionably there was truth in Buddhism. But it was not itself the truth. It taught virtue, but it was patience rather than action, endurance and not enterprise, which it commended. It treated woman better than other Eastern religions, but it did not set her free, in her own place. It could not hold its ground in the country in which it was first known. It has been clearly pointed out that the radical fault of Buddhism was in its selfishness. "It rests on pure individualism; each man's object is to save his own soul." It was overthrown in India, but it left its influence on the country and on the older religions, and it found a home in other neighboring lands, where its believers have been innumerable and its influence immeasurable. But neither in India nor elsewhere has it made, or can it make, such a country as we wish the world to resemble. Buddhism is sadness. It could not establish men in comfort, nor constitute a state. The world needed God, the Maker and Father of men, and He was not seen there. Men knew nothing of his love, of his sympathy and help, and had no thought that they could walk with Him, even in this world which He had made for them. In isolation, egotism, selfishness, there was no escape from their sorrow, and the evil which produced it. This is not reasoning. It is not a homily. It is a result. Man's effort to find God and be at peace with Him had failed, and he was himself the sign of its failure. There was no hope apparent, unless God should come to men and raise them to Himself. Would He do this? Who should say? Buddhism was not in itself a religion. It recognized the gods who had been known in the land, but it had no worship for them. It was willing to worship Buddha, and to see in him the sovereign of life. He was Intelligence, the Enlightened One, and by many such names we may call him. But he was not the Light; a beautiful Star, but not a Sun; not even a planet of the first magnitude, by reason of his lack of light. I must conclude these hints, happy that no more is needed. Yet I shall bridge the way before us with the words of Maurice, whose learning and fair dealing all men respect: "I ask nothing more than the Hindoo system and the Hindoo life as evidence that there is that in man which demands a revelation — that there is not that in him which makes the revelation." I have been interested in the statement in a letter just published, from one of the leading advocates of Oriental belief, that the principal representative in this country of the religious thought of India is not a Buddhist, and that the Vedanta has been taught "as a system of philosophy which might underlie Christianity as well as the religion of the Hindoos."

I am not attempting a history, or even a sketch, of the religions of the world or any one of them. If I were, I should, of course, give a much fuller account of Buddhism, which has admirers among us, and I should go to other nations. It would be of value to study the effect of Buddhism away from its home. It is not unlikely that in its course it received aid from Christianity. Its effects can be traced in Japan, where it helped to raise the people from their low estate. But its work there reached its bounds. That the Japanese have made a great advance upon many lines is evident. A few men have felt in good measure the outer influence which has appealed to their own striving, and wrought with it, and by them the nation has been moved forward. But there is no content in this. Man has not found his true self as the child of God, nor come to the knowledge of his will, in its grace and truth. The nations all bear striking witness to the need of a light which is not of men.

We can form our own judgment. Even with the charm, the spell, of Oriental mystery upon us, we can be sane. I am quite sure I express the common assurance, based upon knowledge, that it is not to India we are to look for the world's enlightening and delivering faith. Not to India with all her own resources, with the benefits of Mohammedanism, even with the influence of England, with the presence of the foreigner in her seaports, with any natural advance which can be discovered, with the teaching of a few Christian missionaries, can we look for the faith which is to strengthen manhood, liberate and exalt woman, promote robust virtue, restore the full divinity of life. When we seek life for the world, it is not there. If not there, where is it?

I wish before I turn from these hurried thoughts upon religious systems to say a word of respect for them, and, if I may, to make them tributary to my main design. Nothing which so deeply concerns the heart of man, and has a real part in his life, can be rudely handled or lightly regarded.

We must all feel the justice of these words of a thoughtful teacher: "Nor do I think any man of modesty or thoughtfulness will ever speak contemptuously of any religion in which God has allowed one good man to die, trusting;" and further, "You will always measure your neighbor's creed kindly, in proportion to the substantial points of your own." Let us recognize with gratitude the efforts of men in the expression of the religious sentiment and in the attempt to make this of service to the world. There is here a truth of the largest significance. It is not the result alone, but the attempt itself, which concerns us. We cannot fail to notice, in the theories and professions at least, the insistence upon morality, the assertion of the authority of the right. The application often offends us, but there is a thought, a feeling within, which deserves regard. "God is no respecter of persons; but in every nation he that feareth Him and worketh righteousness is acceptable to Him." The study of the world's religions is becoming popular, and with good reason. They have been too long neglected and too little esteemed. We should be informed regarding each one, and the relations between them, and any advance which can be found in their thought and influence.

Whatever else they may be, the religions of the world are a revelation of man. They disclose his need and his spiritual nature. If they do not declare a capacity for intercourse with the Divine Being, they do make known his ability to look beyond himself and beyond the world, and to find principalities and powers filling the spaces which enclose the stars. He sees a spirit in nature. If he confounds this with the things he looks upon, and sends his adoration out into the light, or even makes images to represent it, — images which are quite sure at last to detain his thought upon themselves, — this is something of account. It is much when men believe in that they cannot see, and are aware of a life above their own; different from theirs, but sufficiently like it for communion, and some community of interest. They may admire the forces and authorities about them and above them, or only fear them and dread their approach. What they do is of less consequence than that they should in some way think upon them, know that they are there, believe that they can be reached with prayers and offerings; that by sacrifices their anger may be averted and their favor secured. We may call this superstition, but there are worse things than superstition. To see gods everywhere is better than to see God nowhere. Superstition is a perversion, and its forms are often degraded until the truth which is in them is well-nigh beyond recognition. But there remains a point, a germ, of which something can be made. God has not left Himself without witness, nor limited this to "rains and fruitful seasons." Whatever has been the influence of these religious systems, they offer no reason for withholding a fuller revelation; nay, they declare a reason for presenting it, in their insufficiency, and in their witness to the ability of men to be religious. Let us recognize the universal religious principle in man. When a ship is at the pier, you do not know that she will move. When a ship is a hundred miles at sea, it is safe to infer that she will go farther.

Roswell Hitchcock truly said: "Even if religion were altogether a superstition, it is an inevitable and an indispensable superstition." The worship, however poor, of nature, or the power or powers whose form is nature, whose dwelling is in the light of rising and setting suns, — the endowing of nature with personal qualities to which men can address themselves, — are a witness to the far away origin of the mind to which such conceptions are possible and natural. It is the stifled cry of men upon a raft in mid-ocean, when the ship has gone down and no land rises from the many billowed waters, and there is no bread on the unplanted sea. It may be dreadfully low, this superstition of the world. If there was "no gentleman on Olympus," what can be said of the Pantheon of savagery? The likeness of the gods to those who made them is too sad for anything but pity, unless it be hope. We are upon the lowest plane. There are better things farther up. There are noble thoughts, beautiful sentiments, worthy aspirations, brave attempts at a truer and happier life. What revelations the Father of all men has made as the centuries have rolled on, we may not be able to tell. He has not separated Himself from the world, nor lightly regarded any one's need. There is a true light "which lighteth every man that cometh into the world;" a saying as simple and natural as it is rich in promise, and worthy of the place in which it is recorded. The appeal is not to credulous charity and amiable desire, but to a broad reason, a discerning vision, and to our faith in God, the maker of the heaven and the earth, and the man. In the study of our fellow-men, it is required of us that we make the most and the best of all that we discover. It is not strange that when we wander beyond the domain which we have inherited we find little which pleases, and nothing which contents us. The sad, unmistakable fact is this, that the religions, and forms of religion, upon which we are lingering for a moment are not good, even for those who have nothing else. They do not give them the light and life which every man must need; they do not meet the wants of those who cling to them, nor do they promise ever to do this. There is too little truth, and too much error; too little which strengthens, and too much which enervates; too little from above, and too much from the earth. We may regard it as proven, that no religion made by men can do for men that which must be done. Let us not blame men for not doing what is beyond their power. Let us, rather, look up to the hills from whence came life in the beginning. If God is our Father, as we say, He will speak to us. "Adam, where art thou?" when we hear it, summons us to God. I do not see why we may not take life at first hand. God is more easily reached than men; and there is satisfaction when one is learning from Him.

Think what it is which needs to be effected. It is the renewing of a man's life; of his conduct, but more than that — of the stream of life upon which conduct is borne. Life itself must be made pure, godlike, as it was when it came with the breath of the Eternal, with the being of the man. A change so deep and thorough and essential can only be wrought by Him who first created man. I am carrying Virchow's words farther than he intended, but the analogy is close, and analogy in this is not far from argument. Life can come only from life, he said. The life of the soul, the spirit, can come only from the living and eternal Spirit. Here the religions of the world fail. They lack the creative power. Something of truth, of virtue, of spirit, they may have. But not the divine, spiritual vitality, cleansing and quickening the thoughts and desires of the soul. The facts are before us. Efforts at reform are made, notably in India, and by men who are in earnest, and who have apparently rays from the Light of the world, if I may change the figure. But they do not bring their own life or the nation's life to the new Life itself, the Life which is fully the light of men. Religion should be simple, dignified, exalted, evoking the homage which it fosters and rewards. It should promote human life, sanctify the home, enlarge virtue, quicken ambition, promote enterprise, secure knowledge, make the man more and more conscious of himself, and awake to his divine lineage. Little of this do you find where men have been left to themselves. Is there a better test of a religion than the place it gives to woman? Doubtless there are pleasant homes, sacred loves, happy mothers and children, where men have wrought out their own faith. Find as many as you can. Unless our standards are local and inadequate, such things are very far from the rule. Those who have looked longest and most carefully bring the report of little gladness and hope, little liberty and promise; much of sadness turning to despair. I need not here call to mind the Pundita Ramabai whose pitiful tale of her countrywomen has been forgotten by no one who heard it a few months ago. She gave but a glimpse of her India, but it was a native woman's look, and from it came a sister's plea. Only a little of India she disclosed, only pieces of real life. Many remember the prayer of the child-widow which she repeated: "O Father of the world, hast Thou not created us? Or has perchance some other god made us? Dost Thou only care for men? O Almighty One, hast Thou not power to make us other than we are, that we too may have some part in the blessings of life?" I believe there is still an association in Boston which sends New England pity and money for the succor of imprisoned lives in India. Ramabai was seen only a little time ago in the white, graceful dress of her country, with her face radiant with thankfulness, and the inspiration of truth and light covering her. Her tender, eloquent voice was heard in Channing Hall, begging with resistless confidence for a "Faith, Hope, and Love Home" for the women and girls of India. Must it be proved that the misery she asks us to relieve is the result of the religion of the land? I but remind you that the religion of the land has allowed it, and has not removed it, and does not expect to remove it. Shall I say, does not know how to remove it?

To study the world's religions one by one, and with comparison, is of little more than historic use, unless we can discover some principle which pervades them and consents to the varying forms in which it is embodied. The forms are not accidental, but come readily into the character and condition of different peoples. If there should be found a common principle in them, this would not be accidental, but must arise from a common source. I do not think the one principle is hard to find, or to comprehend. It is the recognition of powers beyond men, invisible but real, with which men are in actual personal relation. This belongs in human nature, and can be traced to the origin of the human nature in the divine nature from which the life of man proceeds. With the fact of creation by one Creator out of his own life, beside which there is no other, comes as a simple consequence the consciousness of that life, and the feeling toward its origin. Kept in life by One who gave him his being, what is more likely than that man will feel the presence which surrounds him — a presence uninterrupted since the beginning?

The unity of feeling is of vaster moment than the diversity in which it finds expression. The thinking of the world has not been clear or constant. Behind gods often may be discerned one supreme presence, and through forms grotesque may be dimly detected a thought better than its images. Fetichism has been described as "a superstitious veneration for rubbish." Whence does the veneration come? Even if it be utterly useless, and sometimes much worse, what is its meaning? Is it all the degradation of a better thought? Or is it the blind, very blind, long blind, and blinded instinct of the soul which perforce sees a somewhat past itself? It sees it so very dimly, and expresses its feeling so rudely, that it does not hesitate to wreak its disappointment upon the image before which, when things go well, it is ready to pay homage. Still, a feeling is there which witnesses to somewhat outside of the body.

Some may remember a visit made to us not many years ago by the Zuni Indians. We heard their long stories, translated by their white brother, Cushing, who had learned many things of them. But what was of the highest interest was a sail down the harbor, that they might worship. We landed on an island, and were full of curiosity. The Indians disappeared for a time, and on their return they walked into the sea, and then with a solemnity I have never seen surpassed, under the open sky, careless of all around them, they sang their mystic chant, and threw out upon the air from their uplifted hands the grain they offered to the god of the waters, and let it float away whithersoever he would, for it was his, and he had taken it. That was worship. I do not know by what name they called their divinity. We call Him God.

If we pass to higher forms of religion, we see men turning to the heavens from which come the names of the divinities, and the figure of their quality. There is a beauty in a faith like this, which associates with the sun and the dawn, with fire and light, the powers to which reverence and prayer are due. The divinity is above, out of reach, never fashioned by the hands of men, remaining for ages, and boundless in its riches. Or there may be a larger view which includes the partial visions, and thus stands nearer to the truth. Different divinities may stand for one God. This was at times the thought of the Brahman; but it did not prevent caste, nor withhold its sanction from vice. Against this Buddhism rebelled, with its insistence upon morality and humanity. But all this, and all which we name paganism, cannot dishearten me so much as the poor, broken thought of unseen spiritual forces gives encouragement. It is sad that a man should bow before his idol: it were worse if he did not bow at all. You can take away the idol, and leave him kneeling, and that is a good posture in which to see God and worship Him.

III

THE SON OF MAN IN EARLY LITERATURE

THE SON OF MAN IN EARLY LITERATURE

THIS is 1898. The fixed point "in the files of time" from which the years are reckoned was found in a small and remote province of the empire, and in the night when, in the household of a village carpenter, far from his home, a child was born. Strange things are told of this by men who were near when it occurred. A writer of scientific pretension, then a well-known physician, has related that on that night, while shepherds were watching their flocks, an angel bright with celestial glory appeared, and told what had happened in the town beside their field; and that presently a heavenly host was heard singing into the silence the Gloria in Excelsis. This was certainly remarkable, and the narrative separates itself from common legends, not only by the fact that it was written by that man and at that time, but by its position in a biography whose events are presented in prosaic simplicity and directness, to the intent, as the author states, that the friend to whom he was writing might know the certainty concerning the things wherein he had been instructed. The whole memoir is an excellent piece of literature, and the beautiful beginning will keep its place in the hearts that are young. Let us hope that we may never be old.

I do not see anything in the account of that night in the fields of Bethlehem more astonishing than the very commonplace circumstance that our morning newspaper, on its own showing, went to press eighteen hundred and ninety-eight years after the birth of that child. Reference to that event was made in the same terms this morning in London, Paris, Vienna, Berlin, St. Petersburg, and in every place which has a daily paper. This is not all. For every constitution which shall be adopted through the year, every treaty which shall be formed, every ordinance which shall be issued, every bill of sale that is written, every compact for a game of ball, every letter of the school-girl, will carry those four figures which define its place and measure its distance from that child's birth, of which, outside a few peasants, the world was unaware, and to which it would long be indifferent. Herod the king heard of it and was troubled. Wise men came from the East to worship the new king.

The world was to know Him, and to take that night into its life, and to arrange its affairs around it. Here is something to be thought upon. Learning, intelligence, must make account of the fact which is so firmly and generally established that it passes without observation. I have sometimes said that every candidate for a college degree should be required to give a scholarly statement of all the causes which have worked together to produce the date upon the diploma which he seeks, and of the events which have immediately attended the bringing in of this result. I am inclined to think that, for the first degree at least, this requirement, given in the largest way, would be sufficient. A hasty answer, an ill-considered explanation, could be easily given. But scholars are held to accuracy and completeness. This demand would call for knowledge of history; of discovery and the making of nations; of the change in boundaries and governments; of political and military affairs; of science and its annals; of philosophy and its records; of art and its influence; of education and its methods; of language and its extension; of men and their careers which have been set into the movement of the world; of philanthropy and reform; of morals and religion; of missions and their results; of the Church and the churches. Every department of the University Library would be laid under tribute, and proposals to shorten the years of study would be delayed. After all this, the real explanation might not be discovered.

It is evident that I cannot answer the inquiry which I have started. Nor can I trace the steps by which our chronology has been established. The fixed point is an intrusion, but one that has justified itself. The whole matter of the calendar is both interesting and curious. There are certain natural divisions of time, made by the change of day and night, the course of the moon, and arrangement of the seasons. Yet there were difficulties enough on every side, while the great thing was to find a starting-point. Each nation could easily select one for itself, but this was too provincial to last; and to find a day for two nations, or three, was not easy.

It would seem well-nigh impossible to find any man of whose life any one day could be agreed upon by the people of other nations whose own heroes were thus openly passed by. Imagine such an attempt to be made now! Yet that was done. The Hebrew counted the years from the beginning of the world, a convenient place, to which no one could object on the ground of sectarianism, if the time could be discovered, which seems more difficult now than it was then. The Roman counted from the founding of Rome, which was a natural assertion of his national importance. The Greek was of a different temper and began with the Olympic games, or with that one in which Corœbus gained the first recorded victory, which was a little earlier than the starting-point of the Romans. There are various Oriental methods of arranging the years, as from the flight of Mohammed from Mecca to Medina, or the accession of Yezdegird, or the Council of Tiben. These we need not consider. Nor need we linger upon smaller calendars which were based on various local events. To the system of his country, wherever that might be, the Christian conformed. It was his way, and he was not so presumptuous as to think that the events which were most significant in his thought would work a change so stupendous in the affairs of the world as to displace the systems of time by which they were arranged. It was certainly not to be expected that the Roman government, under whose decree Christ had been crucified, would place him at the beginning of its history. It was long in doing this, but it was done at last. It seems to have come about in this way: The Emperor Justinian had directed that all public documents should be dated by the year of the emperor and the name of the consul; but in our year 541 he gave up the practice of nominating consuls, and it became necessary to fix upon some new point from which time could be measured. The Justinian code of Civil Law, which had just been published, made it, perhaps, seem more important that the matter of dates, with which the laws would have much to do, should be adjusted in a rational and permanent way. Since the Roman law was to be so widely extended, and furnish principles of jurisprudence for many countries and many centuries, it was fitting that the initial point of the new chronology should be of universal value. I do not know that all this was thought of, but it might well have been regarded. The fact that such a point was found and adopted shows that in their action the Romans were wiser than they knew. Now it happened — if we may use such a term for a course of events worthy of wiser direction — it happened that a Roman abbot, who bore the not unusual name of Dionysius, but was distinguished by the epithet Exiguus, probably because he was small of stature, had begun in his tables for Easter to count the years from the birth of Christ. Among themselves Christians had before reckoned from their Lord, but from his crucifixion; now the Incarnation, as it was regarded, was to make the beginning of a new era. This Dionysius was a man of high standing; a Scythian, but renowned in the Latin church for his great learning, which appeared in his collection of ecclesiastical laws, of canons and decretals. But his larger work and extended fame were in this simpler matter of the calendar, in which his thought was to have a far wider and larger range than any one on earth could have imagined. He could not tell with precision the time when Christ was born, and in his computation there is an error of four or five years. That is of no importance here, although it would need to be taken into account in the College examination. But the idea of the abbot was at once popular. The time had come for it. It met a want, and under conditions which commended it. That was in the sixth century, as we now count. The idea kept its place and grew in favor. It was taken into the learning of Bede, or Beda, and advanced with it. Charlemagne gave his influence to its extension, and by the eighth century it was very widely in use, and was still advancing, until it has become established as the fixed point of the world's chronology. I do not mean that there was anything mysterious in this, but that it was very remarkable; an impressive fact of which account should be made. Such facts are of consequence as expressing truths and tendencies in clear and compact form. This was of that nature. The prominence to which Christianity had attained, and the recognition which it had acquired in the empire, prepared the way for this act of homage.

Of course the date has moved with events. But how did it get among the events, and belong with them? It moved with law, language, custom, and it remained when these had been driven back. It stayed wherever it went. Other things changed, but this was as fixed as the course of the planets. We do not need to trace it in scattered syllables and obscure usages; it stands in its own right, and is conspicuous in its dignity and authority. In its universal use it is the perpetual memorial of Him whose birthday it records. No man can date a letter, and think what he is doing, without bringing Christ before his mind. What other fact, in the entire history of the world, is constantly mentioned, and kept in connection with the life of men throughout its whole extent, from centre to circumference; in politics, science, business, religion; in the birth of the child, the movement of the man, the government of the nation? Shall we ask the reason for this? I do not wish to force the evident truth beyond that which is just. But when I regard it as I would any fact of nature, any other fact of history, I cannot avoid the belief, which to me is most grateful, that herein is a divine thought, and that this is one sign of the divine purpose, one witness to the mission of Him who was born at Bethlehem, one promise that his work is to be worldwide and enduring.

We have here the life in which the recovery of man is to be fulfilled. The world has decidedly and permanently made recognition of its opening day. It is a singular fact, to be carefully regarded. My present proposition is this: As the Creator gave to man of his own life in the beginning, and that life has lost its virtue while in man's possession, the Creator has again, in these last times, and by a man, given his life to the world.

We have lingered at the birth of the new man. We are to move on for thirty years and mark his life. Let us remember the simplicity of the event from which we start, and the glory connected with it. Its light is shining upon our path all the day. The record of the life is in books held in reverence in many lands. Special divine illumination and guidance have been claimed for their writers; and in the minds of wise men the claim has been well sustained. Such assistance could readily be given. But the books have their own claims upon our attention and confidence. They offer unusual advantages for the study now before us, in that they contain four separate biographies of Him whose birthday we all regard. There is no parallel for this. There are these sufficiently complete narratives, written independently, after, but not too long after, the life which they present. They were written under different conditions, for different immediate purposes, and with considerable intervals. It is not exaggeration to say that no one living in that time, or within many centuries of it, can be so well known as He whom we have to know if we are to be well informed. Not only the incidents of his career, but his spirit, his intentions, his methods, his character and assertions, his deep thoughts and purposes, are placed before us, in many lights, with varied illustrations, with many repetitions, with an honesty and simplicity which are nowhere excelled. If it is possible for scholarship to determine the importance of any ancient literature, then it has been done in this instance. No effort has been spared, no test has been denied, no research hindered. Reverence and irreverence, the desire to believe and the readiness to doubt, have done their earnest work here. It is a rare tribute to the worth of these biographies that they have been able to draw to themselves the attention of such men as have been enlisted in their study. Think when they were made, to what writers they were assigned, in what land they had their origin, to what subjects they relate, and see that here again is testimony to the value and the integrity of these books. We have no autograph manuscripts, and fortunately none which claim such distinction. But we come near to them, and may come closer. There are tales now and then of antique fragments found in convents and other ruins. But as it is, we come near to men who saw Christ. I do not wish to claim too much, and I am quite ready to accept the conclusions of sincere, painstaking study on all literary questions. The conclusions should be in all respects scholarly; thorough and thoroughly fair, and in the interest of truth alone. But we may well despair of knowledge of the early days if, after all that has been done, these simple treatises are not to be confidently regarded as the trustworthy record of the events in which they claim to have had their origin. I do not care to insist that at every point and in every word they are rigidly exact, but that they are true, as we use that term, and give the truth in simple forms. Their contents might well make us unusually careful, but they should not alter our canons of study, nor invalidate the processes of our reason, nor make us unreasonable in our demands. We may allow for difference of conclusion upon special questions. But when all has been said, the conclusions of scholarly thought find in these pages the true presentment of the life of Him who moves in them.

I speak of these writings as literature. That the books have special qualities, which raise them above other books, I firmly believe. But I do not wish to contend for all which personally I hold to be true and proven. For my purpose it seems best to regard them as the writings of men honest and intelligent, and to read them with the same openness and readiness of mind which we should give to them if they were not concerned with such things as fill their pages. In referring to these writings I have used the convenient term "biographies." This is not entirely correct. In the best sense they are not biographies, with a definite beginning, and a clear and connected account of events, with names and dates, and all the framework of a life. They are such writings as you would expect from unlettered, intelligent, honest men. There is no sign of art, no pretence to literary skill, no obtruding of the authors. Each writer presents the statement of that which he knew, and thought it necessary to preserve and circulate, concerning One who had claimed and received his homage. This is fine, this personal interest and freedom, in which four men prepared four accounts of the one life. Neither wrote a complete memoir, but each did better in describing the life itself; the spirit and purpose which were in more deeds than have been recorded. They wrote from their personal recollection, from common memories of words and deeds constantly recalled, perhaps in some portions from separate records of special events. Their design was to tell as clearly as they could the truths which had become a part of their life, and concerning which error was unreasonable. They did not shut out the light which according to the promise had come to them. They may have learned new words, but they had also learned how to employ words not new. Thus it is said that one of the writers borrowed the term Logos, which he applied to the Master. He was at liberty to do this, if he found the word convenient. The natural question is, not what the word meant where he found it, but what use he made of it in describing the life of One who was the subject of his writing. Read it in its place, as you hear an instrument in an orchestra.

It is a life which is given to us. We find it moving quietly, steadily forward, not more interrupted by lines between events than is the course of a ship by the meridians it crosses. We feel its presence. We are conscious of an idea, an intent, possessing the years, and going constantly on to fulfil itself. Incidents attract and interest us, but it is the life and the purpose incarnate in it which take the strongest hold upon our thought, upon our admiration and confidence. Yet the forms in which the thought was embodied are of great value. We feel the spirit; but the spirit must be manifested in order to be known.

But these records do not stand by themselves. They can be read alone, with nothing before and nothing after them. Even thus they would be instructive beyond all other literature. But no one can read them intelligently without perceiving that they are the extension of writings which were before them. Not to read the entire literature is as if we should study the Puritans without regard to the English history in which they come to light and do their first work. Of all the lives that have been lived, the life of Christ can least afford to be studied in sections, which are regarded as complete. I think that everything which bears the name of heresy rests upon pieces of truth, and not upon truth in its wholeness and variety.

We are chiefly concerned with the modern Testament, properly called New, the New Covenant. All along the way this turns us back to the earlier stages of the thought. The

Master was constantly referring to the Hebrew Scriptures, and showing the vital connection of his life with that which had been written. He could do this, for with the exception of names and dates, the story of his life can be read in the Old Testament almost as well as in the New. His biography was given in advance, even as He said, and his purpose was to complete it. Biography usually follows the life: his also preceded. The tables of his genealogy present an unbroken line, reaching into the earliest days. There is no instance in which this vital connection with the past is more marked than when at the close, at the time when He wished to give to his friends a clearer conception of Himself, and of the work which seemed to be terminated by his death, which had surprised them with its disappointment and startled their faith, He turned their minds back to Moses and the Hebrew prophets and the Psalms, that they might see that all which had happened to Him had been anticipated and intended, and had been carefully written down long beforehand. We comfort the friends whom we are leaving with the future. So did He, indeed; but He encouraged them also with the past, and there He established their knowledge and faith. He appealed to history to convince them of Himself. He took their ancestral hope and gave it back to them alive. To bind together the Old Testament and the New Testament is one of the best things which bookmakers have ever done. They made a blunder when they put blank leaves between them. However convenient these may be for a family record, the story of our family life, there is danger that they will interrupt our thought of the one life which it most concerns us to know.

In the same way it is necessary that we read forward beyond the memoirs, if we are to understand them. What He had taught was treasured in the minds of men who became the teachers of others. Their teaching became another biography, if I may retain that word. They did not invent or discover truth; they repeated it, as they were called to do. One wrote in this way: "That which was from the beginning, which we have heard, which we have seen with our eyes, which we have looked upon, and our hands have handled of the Word of Life. That which we have seen and heard, declare we unto you, that ye also may have fellowship with us." The teaching of another, often thought of as a leader among the disciples, was in like manner the telling of the things which he had seen and heard. In the second letter which bears his name he asserts his authority to declare the power and coming of the Lord: "We have not followed cunningly devised fables, but were eye-witnesses of his majesty." Here is the memoir, declared in the lives of men who knew it, who knew it so thoroughly and believed in it so utterly that it made their life, and commonly their death. The men and the word agree.

The Gospel, as we have come to call it, is not a matter of manuscripts alone, priceless and satisfying as they are. It is a matter of life, active, intense, devoted, at once a passion and a faith. Then, the career of the first apostles was written out by one who was with them. It is not a history: it is a series of annals, the simple narrative of important events. It is the common belief that this man had written one of the accounts of Christ's life, and his warrant for this was in the fact that he "had perfect understanding of all things from the very first." But the Book of the Acts of the Apostles is the extension of the memoir of Christ. It is the story of men who had learned of Him, and were now, in fulfilment of his instructions, teaching the world. It is a declaration of the facts which were afterward written in the Gospels, and were then held in the devoted memories of men who had given their life to the work of teaching them.

But there is more than this, for a man comes

forward who is to be chief in the new work for the world. He had been slow to believe the new teaching. He saw the peril of the old Church, in which survived all the liberty which his people retained. He resisted stoutly all the advances of the Christian faith. He persecuted with extreme severity those who belonged to it. At length this was all changed. It is said that every man goes, at some time in his life, to Damascus — the place of the last decision. Mahomet looked on its delights and sought another paradise. This man fell blinded at its gate and in the darkness found the eternal light; and found himself. He was drawn to the cause he opposed, and became its foremost friend and apostle. The story is told more than once. But besides all that was written, there is the man, a force in the world, a person for history, with a life which compels attention. He was taught the word and work of Christ, and he became himself the teacher of this truth. Opinions were exchanged for verities, and the verities put in command of life. We have his letters, practical letters of instruction, encouragement, reproof, the expression of his great heart, informed by his great purpose. He was stoned and imprisoned, but he never faltered in his understanding of Christ and his words and his life, nor hesitated to tell all that he knew, and he held himself ready to die in this faith, even as it was appointed unto him to do. Beaten three times, stoned once, thrice shipwrecked, a night and a day in the deep, pursued, tormented, he kept to the faith he found at Damascus, proving it in all its promises, and setting his influence deeply into the life of the world. Few men, I do not know that any men, have controlled the world's religious thought more than he. His memoir is in the New Testament. But it is also written with the thinking of the centuries.

Here again is the story of Christ's life, written and unwritten, embodied in the biography of a man, and in the churches which he founded; made a part of the history of the world; the literary, political, religious history of the world. We have the life of Christ when we have the life of Paul, and his addresses and epistles; and the life is the same that is described by the men who saw it.

This man, strong in his character, mighty in his deeds, stands as the permanent witness to the truth to which he gave his life. He was a teacher of religion. Nevertheless, he must be understood by every one who would have a clear knowledge of the course of events in the world. Paul must be recognized. But every thought of him is a thought of One concerning whom he said, "I do not live; but He liveth in me."

But the life of Christ does not stop here. The pervasive principle which marked it was its continuance. It promised to remain with men, to become a part of their life, blending with their thoughts, guiding their conduct; strengthening, inspiring, comforting, without limitation of time. Its influence was of that kind which could be put to the proof, whether Christ was seen or not. I wish to call attention to a fact of the greatest significance. The religion taught by Christ we call Christianity. If Christianity was ever true, it is true to-day. It can be seen at work now, and studied with all care, and without the charming distraction of the Master's presence. He claimed the future. He sent forward his influence. The end of the world, of which He taught, meant both time and place. This forward looking was one of the most marked things in all his teaching. " I am with you to the end of the world," He said. More than that, He commissioned men to go into all the world and offer to every man what He had offered in the three years He spent in Palestine. This was begun while his disciples lived, and has been going on ever since; is going on to-day here and in every land, on almost every island and patch of coral in the seas. Yet if we could gather up the teaching of these messengers it would be found in its essential truths to be the same which is recorded in the New Testament. Indeed, we do gather it up; we know what they teach; and it is what they like to call "the old, old story." It has expressed itself in many tongues and with many forms, but the underlying truths have been the same.

We can find in their words the account of Christ's life; and more than that, the continuance of his life. We can trace the effect of listening to Him, believing in Him, following his instruction. A multitude which cannot be numbered, comprising men distinguished for learning, prudence, carefulness, moderation; for skill in affairs; for generalship and statesmanship; for high thoughts and great achievements; with many of less rank, of plain minds and common lives, give their witness to Him.

There is more than the evidence given in the lives of men. The story of Christ has self-evidencing power. It gains the approval of the reason and the heart. Men feel that it is true. Paul was able to appeal to this and write that by manifestation of the truth he commended himself to every man's conscience, when the conscience was in the presence of God. I have no doubt that there were persons in Corinth who smiled as they heard this daring appeal. But the saints in

Achaia knew that he was right. The knowledge of one man is of more authority than the ignorance of several men.

Nothing that we know is more beautiful than this assurance. Men learn to speak of Christ as a present friend. It does not occur to them to doubt his word. They are simple as children. When one remarked on David Livingstone's loneliness in Africa, he answered that he was not alone. "Christ said that he would be with me always. It is the word of a gentleman of the strictest honor, and there's an end of it." When he fell upon his knees in an African hut, and threw his arms forward on the couch and rested his head upon them, he believed that the promise was kept. The candle burned low at his side, and his heart ceased to beat, but he knew that he was not alone. His weary body lies under the pavement in Westminster Abbey. He won the place. There is no truer shrine among the monuments. Why should he not be believed when he speaks of that which he knew best and cared for most? Unbelief may go a long way and be respected; but there is a limit which it has no right to pass.

I may add that in institutions Christianity has preserved the record of itself. The societies, formed in the name of Christ and around his teaching and Himself, are called churches. I do not mention this as information, but because it is sometimes fancied that there is something mysterious about a church. It is a society of men and women, with its own purpose and endowment, and is as good as the men and women who compose it. It has the highest sanction, and quite as much authority as would be for its advantage. The churches made the New Testament, as a book or a collection of books, containing truths which they knew, and they have preserved it. Their strength to a great extent has been in their adherence to the historical documents of the faith. When their regard for these lessens, there is real and evident danger that teaching will become mystical and sentimental, and decrees oppressive. It is an obvious safeguard to faith and practice, that every man can read the charter for himself and protect his own liberty. Of this independence there is no serious lack in this neighborhood. We might have learned the words of Christ from a society which transmitted them without writing. But we are more confident that the words are correctly given to us when we have also the ancient records.

The churches have also taken special events in the history of Christ and embodied them in forms which have preserved them. Thus the churches are an early witness to the Resurrection of Christ.

His Resurrection is the vital fact, without which there would have been no churches, and the assurance of this fact has not grown less. They have Baptism, by which from the first his friends have been marked as his own. Each instance of this Baptism points back to the earliest. They have the Eucharist, which could never have been devised by men, which has gone everywhere with his name, which his friends keep in remembrance of Him; and this reaches in unbroken succession to his own guest chamber in Jerusalem. Here are great truths, which live by their own force, which are imbedded in the cause of civilization, which owe nothing to history, or to the act of man, save for transmission, and which are only explained by seeing them in their origin. If we question concerning them, we get a variety of explanations; but we always get this, that they are the things to which Christ gave being, and which He committed to his friends, that they might give them to the world. The churches themselves in their existence and their meaning, even in their divine claims, are a witness to Him and to his life; and whatever of usage they have added, they have held Him supreme, and have preserved the knowledge of his word and work.

I wish to call attention again to the surpassing amount of the knowledge of Jesus Christ which is in our hands. Whose life is prolonged as his has been, and shown in so many ways? We have incidents, addresses, conversations, meditations, and prayers; questions and answers; revelations of the heart, of emotions, purposes, desires. More than this, let me repeat that we have the words of Christ embodied in the lives of men, and in their institutions; put to all conceivable test in the heart and the home; in the closet and on the house-top. We can see Christianity in action. The testing is severe. If it cannot make itself known and approved in this way, there is small encouragement in resorting to any other. But who besides Christ has made men of many centuries live around his teaching, more than content to have it the soul and passion of their years? I think that no one has ever lived, even of the men of our own time, of whom we can have this interior knowledge, till not even the beating of the heart is concealed from us.

Think again who He was at his birth and what the chances were that He would ever be known beyond the neighborhood of Nazareth, and say if there be not in this unexampled, unapproached career a purpose which intelligence must apprehend.

Thus far, for the most part, we have gone about the life of Christ. Let me ask you now to look within it, to the end that we may know Him more fully and accurately. The times were ready for his coming. The world was at peace. The nations which were consolidated into the empire offered a fine opportunity to Him and to the work which He was to do. Men were tired of the religions which were unequal to the demands fairly made upon them. The religion of Judea had reached the point where it could pass into larger truth. The period has been well named "The fulness of time."

The place was suitable. Palestine was small and of slight influence. While central among the nations, it was isolated by its position, and by the traditions and the temper of its people. But noted cities had been upon its coast, and there men famous in commerce and the arts had their homes. It had been rich in strong men and great events. The land even now illustrates the New Testament, in mountains and seas, in customs and habits, in food and dress, in ploughs and boats, in the events of nature. It had felt the influence of other countries, at whose hands it had suffered, whose armies had traversed its roads on their way to conquest and defeat. It knew the world, for the world had touched it on every side. It was a persistent, stubborn country, which could be cast down, but not destroyed. Its people could be killed, but not conquered. It considered its own history religious and looked proudly through its misfortunes to its glory. Its religion kept it apart from its neighbors. It worshipped one God, who shared his authority with no divinities, to whom no image could be erected, whose altar no graving tools could touch, whose statutes remain until this day the expression of the duty of man. It had a grand array of prophets, men who stood for Jehovah. Its Scriptures are our own religious books, which is a testimony to their universal character. We sing their songs, and find no better words of praise; we treasure the comfort in their promises, and breathe out our penitence in their Miserere. No other land could have given such words, over which the centuries have no power. Think for a moment what advantage the literature of Greece and Rome had over that of Palestine! In their character, in the position of their people, in the men who were interested in them, the books of either land stood a thousand times the chance of being the chief books in Britain, Germany, America. We do indeed read and admire the literature we call classic, and shall continue to do so, yet only the few know anything of it. The one book of poor, isolated Palestine is the book of the civilized world, the book of church and home and college and school. How this came about is a question of interest to scholars. It has even been said, perhaps not with strict accuracy, that if the Bible should be lost, it could be reconstructed out of the other books into which by portions it has been copied. One thing is certain, a few pages in the second part have carried all the rest into the history and experience of the world. It is to be noted that whatever estimate we may put upon the New Testament, the principles of our religion, the great truths which we cherish, are from Palestine. All this has come to us, not because of Moses and the Prophets, of David and the other Psalmists, but by reason of that Child whose birth we register every day. He explains history, and history in its turn and in its measure explains Him.

It was the breaking of a long silence when there appeared in the wilderness of Judea a man clothed in camel's hair bound about him by a leathern girdle; who called men to repentance, declaring that the kingdom of heaven was at hand, and that One was coming, the latchet of whose shoes he should not be worthy to unloose; who should baptize with the spirit of God. He was the Voice. Thus he called himself, taking his name, not from genealogies which abounded in Johns, and could have given him nothing, but from his calling, wherein at that time he stood alone. Such voices had not been strange in Israel. The utterances of other days we are yet studying. This Voice had itself been foretold, so great was his significance. It was the voice of a prophet which was again heard in the world. It moved men. Strong, severe, commanding, it compelled them to listen. They gathered around the Voice and waited upon his will, which lacked nothing of daring and directness. His words were his own. Echoes are interesting, but not instructive. Such a Voice was needed, and it came at the right time. It prepared the way for the One who was to follow. He preached a new life in a new name, and called men from their old ways into the ways of God. He drew some men closely to himself, and into a jealous friendship, and he did not conceal the fact that he was to be supplanted. To all questioning he gave the same answer, There is One coming. At length He came. It was as it had been said. The former decreased, to find his greater renown in allegiance to another who increased.

I only touch the years here and there, and let the mind move over them. Of the birth of the Child we have already thought. His home was at the North. The house of Mary has been removed. This is evident. But we mark the line between legend and history when we are told that it was taken up by angels and carried to the height of Dalmatia and afterward across the sea to Recanati, in Italy, and at last to the hill of Loretto, where it is visited by pilgrims to this day. It is said to be "the most frequented sanctuary of Christendom." Compare this with the memoirs in which there is not an eccentric line. The home was in the right place. Galilee was an attractive province, with its lakes and hills, its cities and towns, its vigorous people, "healthy as their own climate and cheerful as their own sky," and far enough removed from Jerusalem for the growth of strong and independent character; rugged, perhaps, but free. In a village of Galilee He grew up. It is a fair and flourishing village now. Bethlehem and Nazareth keep their place, while other towns have been lost, as Cana and Capernaum. Nazareth feels the modern life, and the tall chimney of a factory rises above its white houses, which are long seen as one rides across Esdraelon. There was to be no haste, and his life was as the life of other boys; or if it were different, we have not been told. No romance hovers around those years. Some legends have been made, but with legends we have nothing to do, and it is easy to know them. We cannot err in thinking of the home as sacredly pleasant and helpful, and of the child-

hood as beautiful in its purity and promise. We
have allusions to games He may have played
with other boys — the wedding and the funeral.
Two lists of genealogy trace his descent, the one
from Abraham, and the other reaching to Adam
and thence to God. Great names are in the cata-
logues, and in these the boy was instructed at
home and in the village school. Teaching and
learning were not broad in Galilee, but they
included strong characters and large events.
When we limit our estimate to the things which
a man must know, the education of that people
is not to be lightly esteemed. They knew the
better half of science — that God made all things.
The best truth of Astronomy they perceived —
that the heavens declare the glory of God. They
held in their own literature a more accurate view
of the world and its surroundings than was elsewhere to be found. They had the only account
of the creation which was scientifically correct.
Of Psychology they knew nothing, under that
name; but they understood men. Sociology was
well ordered, and was generous and humane. It
had the highest authority. There is very little
in the social science of our day which was not
recognized in the rules of the Hebrew life. There
was not very much history, but the principles
which history describes and illustrates were already

apprehended. Their wisdom is profitable to us, and their poetry has not been surpassed. There was for this boy a special charm in the literature which was within his reach, because so much of it related to his own kindred and the family annals. Imagine his delight at the story of Joseph, which has no rival to this day; and of David, shepherd boy and king. How quickly he learned the Twenty-third Psalm, which He was told his shepherd grandfather had written! Then the matchless idyl of Ruth, the girl of Moab, whose fidelity gave her place in Israel and raised her to renown, — and Ruth was his grandmother. This and many things besides, the neglected Tables tell us.

It was with a mind well stored, and a heart enriched, and curiosity and imagination alert, that when He was twelve years old — and twelve was old then as it is now — He found his long dream fulfilled and was in Jerusalem, the city of the great King. He saw the Temple. He knew what it was, and that is rare knowledge for any age. He stayed behind the company to which He belonged, and was found among the revered teachers of his people; questioning them, as his right was, and answering their questions. He surprised them, whether He asked or answered. He was the Teacher. He knew what they had not learned. The familiar painting is correct in this, that the light is upon Him, and from Him shines upon the heavy faces which bend toward Him. All that heard Him were amazed. He was not. Disappointed He was, I think, that among all the Doctors no one could tell Him what He wanted so much to know, and explain what He had been thinking in the fields around Nazareth. I suppose no one thought of it that day; but as we now see Him standing there, and look into his eyes, and mark the delicacy of his mien and the fineness of his thought, it is quite certain that painful years are before Him, that the world will give Him no sympathy, will not hear his word, will not receive his light, and will try at last to silence his voice. I know that I am reading later events into the story, but I have the right to do this. Indeed, one can hardly help doing it. I do not know why the good physician who has given all we have of this incident in the life of the boy did not tell us more. Perhaps he wrote all that he knew. It is best as it is. We have the few sentences, and can think the rest. There are tenderness and sadness and promise in the closing words. When the Child was found by his sorrowing father and mother, He said, " How is it that ye sought me? Did ye not know that I must be in my Father's house?" It was a new name for the Temple, and a new name for Him. It was an appropriation of the name "Father" which had not before been made. To Him it had profound meaning, and its truth took precedence of all other relationship. It was right, even dutiful, that He should remain at home while Mary and Joseph returned to Nazareth. In his own time He would go to them. "And they understood not the saying which He spake unto them. And He went down with them, and came to Nazareth, and He was subject unto them; and his mother kept all these sayings in her heart. And Jesus advanced in wisdom and stature, and in favor with God and men."

Then followed eighteen years, of which we have no fuller record than has just been given. No mystery comes out of those years, no sign of power, no presage of greatness, no intimation that He will ever come to the place He holds to-day. He was afterward called the Carpenter's Son and the Carpenter; it is probable that the name was truly spoken, and that He had learned that honorable trade, in which He would be useful. There can be no question that his work was well done and according to his promise. We can almost fancy that the willing wood yielded itself gracefully to his gentle hand. Why is there nowhere in the memoirs a hint of this? Because it never was so, and honest men were the writers.

We think of him as quiet, kind, obedient, fond of flowers and birds; familiar with nature;

> Knowing that Nature never did betray
> The heart that loved her.

He was thoughtful, spiritual, — now we should call him dreamy and imaginative. His mind and heart were open to the spirit of grace and truth. He thought most, as afterward He taught most, out-of-doors.

Thus He came to be about thirty years of age. Doctor Luke does not give the age with exactness. Then He began to teach. He took leave of his home, and of his peaceful days, and, with his heart full of great desire, went down to the Jordan, where the new and strange prophet was baptizing. There He found, among the friends of his forerunner, his first disciples. He was Himself baptized, thus coming under the law of the kingdom which was coming into the world. Out from his long solitude He passed quietly into the three long years which were to complete his life. Let me take a few events in their order, that we may be reminded how simple his life was, and how singular, without precedent, and never to be repeated. Let us mark how admirably his life and Himself were adjusted, each to the other. In giving a title to this chapter I have used the term "Son of Man." This name was peculiarly his own. It was made prominent by Himself, when He was here, but no one else employed it to describe Him. It had a Messianic reference. But I am concerned with it now because it expresses his position so clearly. It is impressive to mark his pains to emphasize this relationship to men. It seems as if He was so conscious He was the Son of God that He feared men would not see that He also belonged to them. That they would be impressed by his divine life, and not regard his human condition and experience. I am the Child of Man, He says; not of a man, but of mankind. I am the Son, not a Son, the Son, standing by myself. The Child of the race; The Man, the true man. Thus He continually identified Himself with men, intending in this way to bless mankind. It was only a few days after his baptism, and when He was full of the Holy Spirit, that He was "led by the Spirit in the wilderness during forty days, being tempted by the devil." Who shall venture rudely into those strange weeks! Two accounts are given of them, and one which is very brief in addition. The impressive point is that He knew Himself and the work which He was to do. The temptation was in the line with his work. It was intelligent, and was directed against the purpose which ruled Him and the way of its accomplishment. The temptation was the disclosure of his plan. We see what thoughts were in his mind and what purposes engaged Him. He felt his power. He knew that the kingdoms of the world were to be his. Otherwise the temptation which related to these would have had no meaning. Why should it have been suggested that there was an easy way to authority if He was not seeking authority, and bent upon taking the way that was hard, but which must be trodden if his life was to be fulfilled? As history can be traced in laws, so desire and purpose can be found in this proof of his constancy. One point of contrast should be noticed here. In describing the work of the Son of Man, St. Paul gave him a name not before spoken, but of large significance. He called Him Adam, the last Adam; meaning that He also stood at the head of a race. Let us notice here that under temptation the second Adam, unlike the first, kept Himself down and adhered to the will of God; kept his integrity; held to the work and the way for which He had been given to the world. Compare the trifling in Eden with these words in the wilderness, words of loyalty and victory: "Thou shalt worship the Lord thy God, and Him only shalt thou serve."

Pass on a few days. There was a wedding in Cana, and his disciples were there with Him. Perhaps it was their coming which brought dismay to the house, for it was found that the wine had failed. Though He was a guest, He came to the relief of the household and provided wine. Thus He saved the wedding feast from lasting discredit. It was his blessing on the bride. He was a Man, the Son of Man, rich in gentlest sympathies, courteous and kind. The story is told as simply as if He had brought the wine from the neighboring vineyard. It is told only by that one of his biographers who wrote most fully of the spirit of Christ, of his deeper thought and word. This was the beginning of his signs, sometimes called miracles. There is no mark of wonder. "He manifested his glory, and his disciples believed on Him." As they were on the spot, they had the opportunity to know what was done. Luke does not give this incident, for he was not a disciple, nor was Mark, and Matthew had not then been called. They could have told it from the report of others, but they did not. It was overshadowed in their minds by greater events. It was left for the only annalist who was an eye-witness to describe what he had seen. He wrote like an old man, remembering small things, the number of the waterpots, and their capacity.

A little later He drove the traders and money-changers from the Temple, which again He called "My Father's house." Another could have cleansed the sacred courts. It was a patriot's right. Yet it was remarkable that this young Galilean should take upon Himself such authority in Jerusalem. Only John describes this. I suppose that he was there, and remembered the scourge of cords and the sheep and doves. When there was a similar act three years later, Matthew, Mark, and Luke write of it, but John is silent. He had told his story. It was at the first cleansing that the words were spoken which long afterward were called to mind: "Destroy this temple, and in three days I will raise it up." John understood Him to speak of "the temple of his body."

He was in Jerusalem, and was winning the belief of many by his signs, when at night a man of prominence and of wealth, a teacher and ruler, came to Him to inquire concerning the kingdom of heaven. Why did the ruler come to Him, a carpenter? It was a flattering attention, and would be made the most of by one who wished to be approved that He might gain the people. It was of little use to converse upon the ways of God until the man's heart had entered them. He had to tell him that the kingdom of heaven was not to be reached by the road on which he was travelling. He was kind, but decided.

Quietly and with skill the ruler's inquiry was met and his mind diverted: "Verily, verily, I say unto thee, except a man be born anew, he cannot see the kingdom of God." It must be entered by life, a new life. Three years afterward this Jewish ruler came again to Christ, who had been crucified, and brought a hundred pound weight of myrrh and aloes for his embalming. Only St. John mentions this, as he only told of the former coming. But see what a place the young Nazarene was taking, what words He was speaking, in all simplicity, but with strange authority and impressiveness!

A few days after the night with Nicodemus He was in Samaria, passing through, as the Jews were not accustomed to do, and wearied at noon He rested at the well which one of his ancestors had dug, and which still bore his name, as it does to this day. A woman of the country came to draw water. He asked her to give Him to drink, for she could draw from the deep well. She jested with Him, and soon, as if He had made no request, she heard such words as she had never listened to before. Forget how familiar they are and hear them for the first time, with Ebal and

Gerizim towering over you, and the quiet of a Syrian noon brooding upon the plain. "Every one that drinketh of this water shall thirst again; but whosoever drinketh of the water that I shall give him shall never thirst; but the water that I shall give him shall become in him a well of water springing up unto eternal life." Soon the well and the water had passed from their thought. She had drawn Him away, and He said, "God is a Spirit; and they that worship Him must worship in spirit and truth." "I know that Messiah cometh," she answered: "When He is come, He will declare unto us all things." "I that speak unto thee am He." She left her water-jar beside the well. Her errand was forgotten. A few drops of the true water had reached her lips. She hastened back to the town and bade the men she met come and see Him. They came and begged Him to remain with them, and He did. This was at the beginning of his three years of ministry. In these instances see his consciousness of Himself, his perfect confidence, his clear knowledge of the truth He was to teach, the work He was to do; and of the final result in the accomplishment of his purpose. He was constant, determined. He knew Himself, and understood the life He was to live.

I cannot follow the incidents farther in this

manner. Yet they need to be read together, that we may feel their unity, the one purpose which they disclose, the steady movement of the desire which nothing can interrupt. It is a stream of intention flowing to the sea, widening and deepening as it runs. Let me name a few points, still taking them in their order. In Sychar He said: "My meat is to do the will of Him that sent me, and to accomplish his work." At Nazareth He went into the synagogue, where He had listened from his boyhood, and when He had read from the scroll of Isaiah of One who was to come, who should do for the world what no one was doing or could do, because the Spirit of the Lord should be upon Him, He said: "To-day hath this Scripture been fulfilled in your ears." His old neighbors, his mother's friends, all bare Him witness, and wondered at the gracious words which proceeded out of his mouth. He moved on, teaching, and giving signs of Himself, — thus it is written, — giving sight to the blind and strength to the lame, quieting the storm, filling the net, calling back into the world those who had left it. Even more remarkable were his declarations concerning Himself. Such words had never been spoken, and have not been spoken since his lips were closed. We have heard them so often that we cannot see how wonderful they are. Others have wrought miracles, but no other has ever asserted such greatness of being and authority. "I am the Truth." "I am the Life." "I am the Resurrection." "I give unto men eternal life." Eternal life is to know the Father and Me — this He taught in his prayer. Hence He called men to Himself. Only by having Him could they have his real gifts. "Come unto Me, and I will give you rest." "Because I live, ye shall live." "He that followeth Me shall have the light of life."

Notice in what strong and varied and unprecedented terms He declared his mission to the world. It was to give life. What life? The Divine life — there was but one, that which was given in the beginning; life with its Divine virtue in it.

This consciousness of Himself, this Personality, is most manifest at the end. Before this, and as if He recalled the family Psalm, He named Himself the Good Shepherd, and added new words to the name: "The Good Shepherd giveth his life for the sheep." From any one else this would have been prophecy: with Him it was intention. He did not speak often of his dying, but it was always in his mind. His friends were not able to hear much concerning it, and it was not in their thought as it was in his. Once He spoke of the serpent that was lifted up in the wilderness, and applied the words to Himself. They did not then know all that He meant.

He told his disciples that He must go unto Jerusalem and be rejected and killed. He was transfigured, his face and his raiment glistened, and Moses and Elias appeared and talked with Him of his decease which He was about to accomplish at Jerusalem. He charged the three friends who were with Him to say nothing of this until He was risen from the dead. On another day He took his twelve disciples apart as they were on their way to Jerusalem, and told them that He should be crucified, and on the third day would rise again. He made this into a sacrament of remembrance, and broke bread and poured wine into the cup, as his body was to be broken and his blood was to be shed. That night He was betrayed, and the next day —

> There is a green hill far away,
> Without the city wall,
> Where the dear Lord was crucified.

This was surprising to his friends. They had seen his power and were not prepared for his submission. They knew that every road out of Palestine was open to Him, and they saw Him move steadily to the only dangerous place in the world. They thought that He was to restore the kingdom to Israel, and erect the throne of David; and they saw Him consent to the cross. They did not conceal their disappointment, and had to learn when all was over that He had done as it had been written of Him. Only a day or two before the end He said in the most impressive tone, "And I, if I be lifted up from the earth, will draw all men unto Myself."

It was a sublime confidence. There was a new view of death. It had been looked upon as the defeat of hope, the setting aside of plans, the breaking of life. To Him it was the fulfilment of hope, the advancing of plans, the expanding of life. Where men looked for nothing He saw everything. He kept his assurance to the last. Even on the cross He drew one man to Himself. He died as He had lived, calm, resolved, faithful, committing his spirit to the Father whose will had formed his life.

I have given to this much thought for many years. I do not know it well. The facts are plain, but there is over them a thin veil which has never been lifted. I cannot clearly explain all these things. I am not surprised nor grieved at this. Should we be able to enter into the deepest counsels of Divine Love? The Love itself passeth knowledge, we are told, and we hold it true. Should it not be so in its deepest works?

Explanations are not wanting. But he cannot have thought deeply who is content with them. It is a place for stillness and reverence. The blessing is readily taken. The full reason we must leave with God. We know in part. Let us be glad that all we know and think and trust is but a part. I mark this, the special, profound meaning of his death, in many ways asserted. He had suffered before. No man can know the burden of the years of sacrifice. His soul was exceeding sorrowful, even unto death, before the cross was reached. But not in this was He to give his life for his sheep, save as this was the inseparable prelude to the end on Calvary. I am glad for my own sake that I do not understand this. I am glad for the sake of others that I do not think I understand it. We can, at least, be sure that He was crucified, even as He said, and that He rose from the dead, and ascended from the sight of men.

I have tried to present in a few lines the life of Christ as it is seen in his biographies. I have yet to speak of the life within this, and of its manifestation in word and deed. I do not need to repeat that in Him we have the divine way of accomplishing the Creator's purposes regarding men; of giving life, a new life, to the world. At least, that is my contention. Whatever else He does for us, He has done this. Whatever other forces work for this end, this is the appointed power whereby we are to be raised to ourselves and our true destiny. Man is to have a new gift of life, in which all he has learned will have its place; his affections, his virtues, his accomplishments, his earnings, all that is good. We have gone far enough to see the grandeur of this Divine presence; the greatness of its Personality; the unprecedented claims and proffers which attend it; the unfaltering purpose which rules it, consents to death and conquers it; and all that it may glorify God upon the earth, and finish the work He has given it to do.

IV

THE PURPOSE AND METHOD OF CHRIST

THE PURPOSE AND METHOD OF CHRIST

It is in Jesus Christ that the Creator has given to the world a new and personal force for its recovery; that man may regain himself and secure the life of honor and strength for which he was designed. In studying this Divine purpose it has seemed best to dwell upon the life of Christ and that which it contained; to the end that we may be impressed with its eminent fitness for the mission to which it was appointed. I have already presented his life in some of its incidents and relations, and I desire now to enter it more deeply. He desired to have this revealed to men; that even his heart should be open before them. His nature was disclosed in acts. The Word unveiled Himself in words; in thoughts, too; intentions, emotions, which He would not conceal. Even his prayer at the foot of his cross was heard of men; his cry in the agony of Gethsemane; his thought and feeling in his crucifixion. All that his friends could receive

He gave to them, and as He went away He promised even more knowledge of Himself, and this they have given to us.

> And so the Word had breath, and wrought
>   With human hands the creed of creeds
> In loveliness of perfect deeds,
>   More strong than all poetic thought ;
> Which he may read that binds the sheaf,
>   Or builds the house, or digs the grave,
> And those wild eyes that watch the wave
>   In roarings round the coral reef.

The study of the life of Christ in recent years has brought Him nearer to us. We have seen Him among men, revealing Himself, letting us look upon his design as it touched the lives which were around Him. We have made use of the privilege afforded us to know Him, and in this we have lost nothing of reverence and admiration, and have gained something in obedience and love.

In all that we see and hear there stands forth the Personality which calls for homage. He is above all which He does. He is greater than his life. To judge what He did and said apart from Himself can only result in confusion and misconception. Let us not fail to mark his constant pains to have us comprehend the truth of his being. He is grieved when men are content with what He does, and do not take Him; when they want loaves in the wilderness, but do not care for Himself, the Bread from heaven. "I" is of necessity the most prominent word in all the accounts of his life. He knows and asserts his relation to God, whom He calls "The Father," and "My Father." He knows that He has come from Him. There are no terms which describe this perfectly. It is plain that every time He speaks of it his words mean too little. There is a mystic tone which reminds us of their insufficiency. "Believe Me that I am in the Father, and the Father in Me." "That all men may know the Son, even as they know the Father." "I do nothing of Myself, but as the Father taught Me, I speak these things." "I and my Father are one." "My Father is greater than I." "All things that the Father hath are mine." "And this is life eternal, that they should know Thee, the only true God, and Him whom thou didst send, even Jesus Christ." "That they may all be one; even as thou, Father, art in me and I in Thee." Let me read one more sentence, and this from the first of the Gospels. "All things have been delivered unto Me of my Father: and no one knoweth the Son, save the Father; neither doth any know the Father, save the Son, and he to whomsoever the Son willeth to reveal Him."

These things were spoken, were written, were believed, and they are in keeping with the life into whose years they are set. They are in place in one life, but not in any other of which we have knowledge. I pray you to mark the presence of this consciousness of oneness with God. Even if the words are not given precisely in the form in which they were spoken, syllable by syllable, I cannot doubt that they present thoughts which He expressed, and which are so impressive that they could not readily be changed, or lost.

I do not wish to speak of this now. But if we are to study the life of any one, his words are a large part of the material at our command. With thoughts like these in his mind, how could it be otherwise than that the whole life should be pervaded by them? Thus we find it in its entire course, and it is never so manifest as in his last hours with the friends whom He is to leave in the world to teach the things learned of Him, and to advance the work for which He has given Himself. We shall do well to read these verses with this intent, that we may mark his consciousness of the life of God. It was of this that He was to give to men. I have no theological phrases or purposes; for it is only the fact in its simplicity which is now before us. Gratitude and hope hail this coming of life to give life to the world, and may well be satisfied. If life is to come it must be from above. As it was the first time, so must it be the second time. The Creator must be the Saviour for his own sake and for our sake. Who shall presume to rescue and restore the work of God? If one may compare two things which are impossible to men, it would seem to be easier to create the world than to save it; once to make a man in the divine image than to make him the second time when the image has been broken and its value lost. The good intention it may not be hard to discover. It is the power which is lacking. Hence we rejoice with great joy, not merely over this life of wonderful beauty and lofty desire, but over a life which has come out of heaven, and whose sources of strength are in God, and are exhaustless.

In what terms shall I describe the relation of Christ to God? I have studied his life, considered his words, observed his influence, marked his place in the world, felt his presence, and received the witness of those who in special intimacy have walked with Him. My own conception of the Person of Christ is as exalted in form as I can now have it, while I am assured that He will be more and more glorified in my thought as the centuries grow.

Personal interest is not to control one's judgment of truth. But it is to me a cause for profound gratitude that here my belief and my interests, my desire and my conviction, are entirely in accord. I am speaking for myself, and not another, and not venturing to measure any one's contentment. It may at least be said that the greater Christ is, the richer are those who call Him friend. I ought in honesty to present this result of my own study, attended with the prolonged testing of confidence and experience.

Yet for my design in these pages, I prefer to give you the statements of others, and of those not of my own theological school, but of the wider fraternity of Christian men. I think I can do no better than to repeat the words of the late revered preacher to Harvard University, whose life was so strong that many churches desired it, whose spirit was so gentle that many churches claimed it. If any one can mediate between variant opinions and expressions, it is Dr. Andrew Peabody. These are his words, spoken in King's Chapel: "We have in Jesus Divine humanity, God manifest in the flesh, God in Christ, all of God that can be incarnate, all of God that we can fully comprehend," "all of the Divine that is communicable." "God in Christ is the only God that the Christian knows." To this I may add the remark of President James Walker: "We see in Christ what we worship in God." The Greek Fathers with their insight saw in Him the "intensified presence" of God.

But the life of Christ is not related to the Father alone. It is in vital relation to men also. The life is in a man. He carries the life of man through to the end. The man is born, he lives, he grows, he dies, and is entombed. The eternal Word became flesh, and dwelt among men, and they beheld his glory. This is written. Living thus among them, He blessed them. He gave Himself and his own life, in sympathy, guidance, comfort, light, and life. He was so near to them that He could touch them. Men touched Him, and drew away strength. Virtue came forth from Him. Light flashed from his fingers into nighted eyes, and health was plucked from the fringe of his garment. When his bidding fell upon the storm it dropped into quiet. Thus it is told by men who were there. He was the Good Shepherd, who must be with his flock, where they can see Him, and know his voice; where He can defend them, and if need be give his life for them. He must be able to go up the mountain if one has strayed, and take it upon his shoulders, and bring it home where He can rejoice over it. All this He was. Indeed, He asserted a more intimate relation with men, whom He called sheep.

It was an old name for them, and in that land an affectionate name. Strangers blamed Him because He extended his favors to men whom they disapproved. "You would do the same," He answered. "If one of your sheep was lost, you would go after it." "Yes, my sheep," they thought. "Well, these are my sinners and my publicans." Thus He claimed men, as if they were his. Were they not his? But He went farther than this. The shepherd is, after all, external. "I am the vine," He said; "ye are the branches." This was to his friends, but it was the word they were to pass on. Now, the vine gives its own life to the branches. The branches are the vine, extended, multiplied. If its life is Divine, their life becomes Divine, for it is this which it has to impart. An Italian monk, a poet, has called attention to the fact that this is all the vine can do. It cannot give beams for a house, nor timber for a ship. It can only give its life, that is, itself. This may be pressing the figure unduly. But it is certain that it was this which He gave, and, in comparison with this, He gave nothing beside. For what were bread, and eyes, and health to be mentioned with his own life! Indeed, He left all illustration when He said, "Because I live, ye shall live." See where in his consciousness He stood, bringing from the Father the life which was his own, and bestowing it upon men, that they might live as the children of God.

I wish that I knew of some stronger terms in which to describe his devotion to men. The facts exceed all statements. We need to avoid all thought of otherness, as if He was between God and the world. We are not to regard Him as separate from us, standing apart, near but remote; only a messenger from heaven, or, perhaps, the very grace of heaven. He was in the Father and He was in the world. He believed in the world. The earth itself He had made — thus the New Testament teaches. In our statements creation is often ascribed to the Father Almighty; but the Gospels and the Epistles present the Son as the Maker of all things. He would be interested in the world which He had made and was holding together, and in the events which were wrought out upon it from the beginning. There was nothing here which did not in some way touch Him, because of his relation to the Father of men and to the men themselves who were his kindred, both in their Divine nature and in the manhood which was his. In Him the Father came to men and was among them. In Him men came to the Father, commended by his brotherhood. For thirty-three years He lived among men. One who knew Him well applied to Him the words of the prophet regarding the Messiah — "Himself took our infirmities, and bare our sicknesses." Another, whose name we do not know, wrote that He was "in all points tempted like as we are, yet without sin." Indeed, his connection with man was all his own. It has been truly said that He was the only man of the race who chose to be born into it. He came for a purpose. Mark how thoroughly He was involved with the world, carrying it always upon his heart. He longed to see it at peace with itself and its Maker. He rejoiced over every good man, over the return of every wanderer, and every sign of better things. He was grieved over its wrong-doing, its insincerity, its selfishness. He knew that He had come to set it free from the evil, and to establish it in righteousness. He knew that this would cost Him his life, but He was willing it should be so. To die, and yet to fail among his own people was hard, for his love and desire were strong. He loved the city and wept over it — "If thou hadst known!" "O Jerusalem, Jerusalem, how often would I have gathered thy children together, even as a hen gathereth her chickens under her wings, and ye would not!" He held men in his heart and named them with Himself. He taught them to say, "Our Father which art in heaven," and if, for Himself, He never said

"Our Father," still after his resurrection He did speak to his friends of " My Father and your Father," as of "My God and your God." This is more than " Our Father " would have meant, in its disclosure of a special power to be used for man's advantage.

The name Jesus was a personal designation. It is found in the Annunciation to his mother, and was appointed because of its appropriateness. " For it is He that shall save his people from their sins." The name Emmanuel was recalled from Isaiah, but was not afterward applied to Him, so far as we know. In the Gospels Christ is an official name, and is more precisely rendered " the Christ," or the Anointed. He seldom used this name. He said, "One is your master, even the Christ." The two are well joined in this passage; Simon Peter said, " Thou art the Christ, the Son of the living God." And Jesus answered, " Blessed art thou." They are found in another form in the Prayer: " This is life eternal, that they should know Thee, the only true God, and Him whom Thou didst send, even Jesus Christ." When we pass to St. Paul's writings Christ has become a personal name. In this the office takes the place of the man, who is known by his mission and work. To be the anointed of God is evidently much more than to be the Son of Mary. Which name we shall use is chiefly a matter of personal preference. It is natural to retain the name in the Gospels. But we are more accurate, historically, when we call Him Christ, and this is more in keeping with the name uniformly given to his friends. Yet both names are to be regarded. For Jesus, with all the glory of his birth, the beauty of his youth, the strength of his manhood, the sublimity of his death and resurrection, was the anointed One. Upon Him descended the Holy Spirit, in Him dwelt grace and truth. When we have Jesus clearly and permanently in our minds we are prepared to see Him "The Anointed," at once the Son of Man and the Son of God. The influence of Christmas will preserve in a delightful way the Child Jesus. Our elder knowledge, treasuring the tender faith of childhood, must see Him who was born in Bethlehem anointed with grace that the world may be blessed with the peace of God.

It was in the fulfilment of his mission as Christ, the anointed, that He preached the Kingdom of God, or the Kingdom of heaven. He knew well what the Kingdom is. It stands in the will of God. It is the extension of the principles by which heaven is constituted. When these are established on the earth the Kingdom of heaven is here. It is in its last analysis the nature of the

Eternal expressing itself for the governance of those who have his life, and responded to by their nature which is of his. Whether in heaven or on earth this is its essential character. The Kingdom of God among men was meant to be as simple, natural, constant, as among trees and stars. As it was preached by Him, it was to be composed of men who had received the Divine life and were to keep it in the rule of heaven. When one man, or one company of men, is placed under these rules, the Kingdom has come. It is within a man when he brings his thoughts under its control. It is among men, wherever there are those who live in the obedience of God. Many do this. More will do it. It is the consummation of human hopes. In it is the magnificent expression of Christ's desire. There is no hindering mystery. There is no difficulty, no complication, when men desire this. It does not involve disorganization, but purification and uplifting. It is not meat and drink; yet it requires the industry which covers the fields with grain, and brings streams of water from the hills. It is "righteousness, and peace, and joy in the Holy Ghost." That was the definition which St. Paul sent into the Empire. It requires kings and all who are in authority to fashion their laws after the will of God. It would bring all business, and all social relations, under the Sermon on the Mount. It requires honor, service, charity. All are called into it: the poor, the prodigal, the rich, the prudent, the near and the distant. It is every man's kingdom and country. This He taught. He was plain, but patient. He sought the beginnings and then would trust them as leaven and seed. It was thus in nature, and this was nature. That which He wished to secure would be gained if men would obey Him. He would have it begin with his own people, but it was to fill the world. No countries are named in the Lord's Prayer. In the Beatitudes those whom He blesses possess both heaven and earth. It was an eternal Kingdom. To leave the world could not remove one from it, for in his thought heaven and earth are one. The citizens of the Kingdom would all be brethren, possessing the Divine life, knowing a common descent and cherishing brotherly sympathy and affection. They would be united by blood, and this would be thicker than anything else that flows. The world would be really the Father's house, or a portion of it, and the family life would grow within its walls. He taught the prayer which we still repeat, not always realizing how deep are the words we say, and perhaps not always consenting to them for ourselves, — "Thy Kingdom come, Thy will be done." It is the divine summons to loyalty. Is not this the purpose we have traced, to bring men to God, to give the second time the Divine life?

"The Kingdom of heaven is at hand" was the cry which preceded his appearance. The King had been sung by psalmists and announced by prophets. He accepted the royal office, declared the royal authority, set up the Kingdom in his own name. Abraham had begun a nation. Moses had restored it. David had given it solidity and extension. But the kingdom of God was not then in the earth, save in a few devoted hearts, and in a purpose which could not be disturbed. The herald had declared his approach, but had disturbed nothing except the wrong-doing in the lives of men. He said no word of politics, removed no business, left men to plant the field and sail the sea, to collect tribute and defend the country as before. But He called for unselfish lives, for integrity, and quietness, and contentment. He would break up all shams, demolish insincerity, and by making the hearts of men clean prepare them for the coming King, in whose rule they would find uprightness and all good. No one could be in it who was not loyal, and no one was loyal who was not good.

The King came. The Psalm had announced

Him as afterward the Epistle named Him and described his rule — "Thy throne, O God, is forever and ever; and the sceptre of uprightness is the sceptre of thy Kingdom. Thou hast loved righteousness, and hated iniquity."

There were upon Him none of the signs of royalty, though his birth was with more than regal splendor. But its reality was there and He soon made this felt. For He was anointed with the oil of gladness above his fellows. He asserted authority over the minds of men and over their hearts, and made their destiny turn on their loyalty to Him. "Ye did it unto Me." He ordered their lives, instructed their thoughts, diverted their purposes, changed their beliefs, startled their religion, revealed their life to come. He began his new Constitution with the Beatitudes, as the Ten Commandments called to remembrance the favor of God; but He ended with a standing or a falling house; standing or falling as it obeyed or neglected his teaching. He gave honor to those who had been before Him; from a child they had been his heroes. But, when He would, He boldly set aside their words; "Ye have heard . . . But I say unto you." He took two commandments from their obscurity, covered with a mass of regulations, and gave them spirit and life for all time. He stretched his rule into eternity. With the wealth, and power, and virtue of a king He bestowed his impartial benefits, and made men feel even here the blessedness of a reign which should be forever, in "the city and commonwealth of God," — "a community whose service is simple righteousness, and whose patriotism is an inexhaustible love of perfection."

There was no display. He moved quietly through the few months which were allotted Him. At the close He came from Bethany into the Capital, the city of David, as He had never come before. A great company attended Him. A multitude from his own North country, who had come to Jerusalem for the feast, went out to meet Him, and hailed Him with their hosannas. They spread their garments in the way, and cast in his path branches from the trees. They cried as He rode on, "Blessed is the King that cometh in the name of the Lord: peace in heaven and glory in the highest." He came as a king, because He was a King. Only once, and it was Sunday, He let the world see his royalty. So once He had stood on Hermon, and his face shone and his garments glistened. That this was but once, and that never anything resembling it came at another time, is a witness to its truth. If any writer had desired to clothe Him with splendor it would have been done twice. The restraint is testimony. At all times submissive, meek, and lowly, He consented to be transfigured; He consented to be enthroned. It was enough for revelation, and it was soon over. Then He wept before the city, and the people cried, "Crucify Him!" The world crucified Him. Europe condemned Him to the cross. Asia furnished the cross to which He was nailed, as it had desired. Africa, land of servants, gave a man to bear the cross when He sank under it. The inscription in three languages proclaimed Him King of the Jews. The title pleased no one. If all after King had been omitted, the writing would have been with dignity. Pilate answered to the men who complained, "What I have written, I have written." That was evident, but he had not written anything, except Jesus of Nazareth.

The crucifixion was thought to be the end. The multitudes who had been brought together by the spectacle went their way, smiting their breasts. Priests and rulers breathed more freely when his reproving presence was at length withdrawn. The hearts of friends were in despair. The mother had given herself into the keeping of the disciple whom Jesus loved, and they lived in the affection of the Cross. The new tomb received its earliest tenant. It was in a garden, as it was in a garden that the need of a sepulchre began, even as it had been foretold. The stone kept the door, and the seal kept the stone, and the guard of soldiers watched before the deserted house. "Make it as sure as you can" was the permission and command. But nothing was ended, save that the method of the life which moved among men was changed. Its works were not undone: the blind retained their sight, the lame walked; the young man was seen on the streets of Nain, and the ruler's daughter gladdened her father's house; while Lazarus passed when he would between Bethany and Jerusalem. The words lived in the fulness of their truth — commandments, promises, revelations. The Lord's Prayer, the Beatitudes, the Ten Commandments, parted with nothing of their force. The air was full of the life He had breathed into it.

In his thought there was no change, no rest, as his purposes, often declared, went on to their accomplishment. More firm than heaven and earth, his sayings could not pass away. The last night with his disciples, the night of the Passover and the Eucharist, was glorified with his unfaltering, increasing design. Never had He spoken so fully of Himself and his intent. He knew that a few hours would bring Him to the cross. But with a confidence unparalleled; clear, steady, generous, loving, Divine; He looked through the clouds of death and saw his life in its Divine and eternal triumph. "I have overcome the world." "O righteous Father, the world knew Thee not, but I knew Thee; and these knew that Thou didst send Me; and I made known unto them Thy name, and will make it known; that the love wherewith Thou lovedst Me may be in them, and I in them." Here was more than submission and more than courage. Here was the clear consciousness of his life and its design, and the certainty that these would pass victorious through all which awaited them; nay, more, that they would be fulfilled in the very events which to the world appeared to thwart them. His confidence remained through all the dreadful hours. It was perfect, even upon the cross.

He was the King, and He knew that his kingdom was coming, and He knew the way of its approach. It was as plain as the road over which He passed on the day when the inconstant world hailed Him with its hosannas. When his kingdom covers the earth, the needed restoration of man to himself and to his Lord will be established. For this the world waits. It is wise only when it beholds the method of God, and sees in his Son the King whose reign is in righteousness and mercy. Whatever agencies may serve his thought, whatever kings may move in his train, by whatever influences He may be assisted, in nature and in the will of the world, He alone draws men to the Divine life which is life indeed. His force is even now bringing in this result. I have allowed myself for a moment to anticipate that which is to come. I have done this lest in studying the life of Christ as it was upon the earth we should lose sight of the meaning of it, and of the end toward which it is advancing.

In returning to the history itself, it is evident that the teaching of Christ and his life are adapted to all times and all lands. This is seen to be true in the nature of things, but it has also been abundantly proved. In his Personality He is at home anywhere, while his words are readily applied wherever they are taken, and they have been taken into all the world. There are no marks of nationality. The illustrations, as given in the parables, are appreciated everywhere. Even while He speaks so often of a kingdom, He does not give his approval to any particular form of government. Every land has its political life and institutions and will understand the terms He uses. But He does not disturb the sovereignties of the nations. His kingdom might be in a republic, or in a monarchy, under emperor or czar, or the head of an island tribe. He would bring the emperor or the chief under his rule and thus administer the interests of the nation. This has been found practicable, for the kingdom is already established under every form of political arrangement. It embraces all sorts of good men and all kinds of honest and useful work. It needs every man, and offers to every one a chance to earn the daily bread for which He prays, and doubles its value with the sweetness of industry and honesty. He gave broad principles of living, wherein class would not be at variance with class. Differences of judgment, apparent differences of interest, would be referred to the king, and would be settled under his direction. His rules honestly administered would be found adequate to the work required of them. It is true that He once refused to be a judge or adviser when two brothers quarrelled over an inheritance. There was no need of his interference, and if the men knew his teaching they knew the rule by which their dispute should be settled. He is really a Prince of Peace wherever men and nations order their ways by his principles. The highest arbitration makes Him the King and his laws supreme.

An eminent judge has recently said: "A very perfect administration of justice would be found where the courts had no contested litigation to decide, because their counsellors and attorneys were so learned, so assiduous, so disinterested, so frank, so fair, and so faithful as to induce all clients to do justly and to submit to right." This was in recognition of the virtue of a lawyer of high rank of whom it was more directly said, " He sacrificed himself, he labored for others, not as in obedience to a stern law-giver, but with the sweetness as of a Catholic saint." A character like this of my friend and classmate, Christ would create in every lawyer and in every man.

His rule enlarges manhood and extends freedom. He would break all chains and have men free indeed, living in intelligence and uprightness. Hence He fosters schools and churches, and promotes all useful learning. He is true to his own nation in this, for there were schools for education in Judea " long before Plato had gathered his disciples round him in the olive grove, or Zeno in the Portico."

His rule encourages art, which had warrant in tabernacle and temple, and all which belonged to them, and still more in the world which had given its imagery to the Scriptures. He let men see the world, and know it, and He nurtured their love of the true and beautiful. More than all, He furnished in the incidents of his own life the choicest themes for music and painting. It is not by chance that the art of Christian lands is most prized, both for its skill and that which it portrays.

The head of his kingdom is the ideal King, sovereign in authority, righteous and generous, living without fear and ruling without compulsion. His banner over us is love. Patriotism is a department of religion, for the King is Divine. Citizenship is worship. In a republic voting is religious. The holy city rises from the earth to meet the holy city descending out of heaven. He enjoined no form of speech. The tongues of Babel were not to be one tongue, but the hearts of Babel were to be one heart. Many tongues were heard at Pentecost, and the Bible is already written in the languages of the earth. Learning has done some of its best work in translating his words, and in this has honored them and exalted itself.

His teachings are not affected by the advance of learning. He gave no opinion and no instruction upon any question of science. The recent advances do not affect any truth He taught. There is something fine in the serenity, the delight, with which the Christian watches the study of nature, joins in it himself, finding in it more and more of the thought of God. One of the leading scientific men of our time, who had once been confused in his faith, has said to me, "My study of nature made me a Christian." He wrote also, "In my own mind, the doctrine of Christ is the summit and crown of the organic series. It expresses the final result of that directed striving which began millions of years ago." It may be remarked farther that Christ gave no instruction upon literary questions. He knew the Old Testament Scriptures and gave them his sanction. But He did not give instruction regarding authorship, dates, and places. He did indeed refer to Moses and the prophets and the Psalms, and show that these spoke of Him, and He pointed out things concerning Himself. But He did not name the authors of the Psalms, or explain the composition of the first books of the canon. There is room here for our highest scholarship, and when its work is done there will remain unanswered questions. Yet we shall continue to find the wisdom which Timothy found, and to know that every scripture inspired of God is profitable.

Take the teachings of Christ where you will, into any school, into any land, and they will keep their place. Light may break forth from them, but it will only bring out their truth. If a fire should burn within them, the bush will not be consumed. They have the permanence which is needed in the prolonged work which they are to do, if they are to help recover the world. His thought and intent, his precepts and promises, were independent of all boundaries. The new idea of God was final. The centuries of study have added nothing to it. God is love, and He is our Father. Worship was enjoined in the only needful way and has never been improved upon. The words at the well of Samaria stand as its highest and broadest exposition. The law was universal. There was no fixed series of rules, no tabulated directory of conduct. Life was to be natural, and the nature was to be love. For method it was taught that the rule of life is, "Not to be ministered unto, but to minister." He went so far as to add what was recorded long after his ascension, that "It is more blessed to give than to receive,"— a truth which we may yet come to accept. We are complacent because we think that the rule of service, of finding our good in another's good, is of our invention. In a lapse of memory we have gone so far as to give this a new name. It is simply a principle taught by Christ. His statement is stronger than ours, and larger. For the service is to be of the heart. It is the second Commandment which is like the first. The love of man in the order of duties comes next to the love of God. It could not come first, for it has its origin and support in that which precedes it. It was needless to call it altruism when it is merely a department of Christianity. One of the disciples challenges all our thoughts of humanity in writing that he who does not love man does not love God. Christ's definition of neighbor is large. He is the man who needs you. He may not be of your town, or nation, or able to make return. He is perhaps lying by the roadside between Jerusalem and Jericho. He may even be one who has robbed you, and left you to die by the wayside. How puerile our modern notions of philanthropy appear when we read the New Testament! That man who turned from the persecutor to the apostle explained the Christ law of love. It hopes, believes, endures; it never fails; it surpasses learning and sacrifice; it is greater than faith and hope, as the tree is greater than the seed. If we are learning this, our teachers are Christians and they learned of Christ.

His teachings concerning money disclose his method. He had no one rule for this. He held money in high esteem, as every honest man does. Some should have it, for its uses; others are called to service in which they do not need it. A young man who was very rich came to Him asking after eternal life. His conduct in general was admirable, and drew out commendation. Two things were required of him, and the two stand together:

"Go, sell that thou hast, and give to the poor; and come, follow me." Perhaps the man's heart was hampered by his wealth, and he needed to be freed; or it may have been only that he was called to close discipleship, and, as a rich man, would be out of place in the little company of those who walked with Christ. He could hardly attend the Master in his walks, and become an apostle of his kingdom, while he was engaged with real estate at Perea. The young man heard the reply, and was offended. He had discovered himself, and he went away sad. Whether he returned is not told. He was disappointed, for he did not like the man whom he had found in himself, to whom his property beyond the Jordan was worth more than eternal life.

Thus Christ met one case in which money was involved. But to a man who had acquired wealth by dishonorable means Christ gave no direction like this. He was content that the publican should make fourfold restoration of that which he had wrongfully taken; and for what was left, let him use it as a Christian. One principle covered all cases. On his last visit to the Temple, He saw a woman casting two mites into the treasury. It was a large gift, for she had nothing left. The measure of a gift is in what is kept. Christ commended her. Would He then have every one cast all his property into the church treasury? By no means. A man has no right to throw the care of it upon others, or to deny himself the blessedness of giving with his own hand. Let the man devote himself, which includes all that he has, to God and his guidance, and give and keep according to his will.

He gave a high value to everything which was done in love. I have never heard of any one who appreciated every favor, however small, so much as He. You give a cup of water to a man in his name, and it will appear to your credit in the Day of Judgment. His memory of love holds every loving thing we do. "Inasmuch" has become the chain by which reluctance is drawn into Christly service.

The whole life of Christ was healthful, simple, — natural. I confess that I like the word. He was thorough, yet we do not call Him an extremist, or think Him radical and visionary. He believed in life, and enjoyed it. He was not an ascetic in any degree. He did not seclude Himself from men, but walked among them, and sat at their tables. His herald in the wilderness had a life of austerity. This well became him. But Christ began his miracles at a wedding, and saved the marriage feast. His works took a common form. He fed men with bread; He saved the fisher's boat; He gave the palsied man strength to carry home the bed he lay upon. They called Him the friend of publicans and sinners, and the name pleased Him. He always liked the truth. His parables interpreted common things; sparrows, grass and flowers, leaves and seed, money and pearls. He gave a new value to all which men handled. There is no great teacher who approaches Him in this use of common things, in the hallowing of the ways of men, in the ennobling of our daily life. He made nature a constant parable, and the pursuits of men were continual object lessons. No thoughtful man could fail to be reminded of God and his ways with men. The world of nature and life is an illuminated manuscript written over with the truths of the Spirit.

Plainly all this is suited to the world. There is nothing which belongs in one clime and not another. No age lessens the value of his words. Our advances in the principles of living are nothing more than learning of Him and consenting to live by his precepts. We do not always confess this, but it is always true. We do not always know this, but we could know it if we would. It is evident that here were wonderful truths with which to go into a restless, discontented, disappointed world.

I have often spoken of the teachings of Christ. It has not been common to regard Him as a Teacher. It is remarkable that while the Greek word Didaskalos is used nearly fifty times in the Gospels with reference to Christ, our English revisers only twice translate it Teacher — when He Himself says, "One is your Teacher," and when Nicodemus calls Him "a Teacher sent from God." In all other places it is rendered Master, a definition not given in the best Lexicon. This is in accordance with the English use of Master, which is higher than that which prevails in this country. Yet very frequently in the Gospels Christ is spoken of as teaching. "He opened his mouth and taught them" was true every day. His teaching is spoken of by that name in the Revised Version of the Gospels, although this before was rendered doctrine. After a time the thought of Christ as the Teacher lost its position in the minds of men, and his work as Saviour was made more prominent. The Teacher disappeared from the ranks of ministers and the priest came forward. This was long ago, but the influence has remained. In our own time, when some insisted that his chief work was as a teacher, and that to follow his instruction was all that any one needed, those who believed that his work as Saviour was of infinitely larger moment presented Him as the Redeemer of the world, and denied to his instruction in itself any such value as was claimed for it. As we see now, the true way was to receive Him as Teacher, and then to receive the teaching. We seem to be recovering our ground. Our conception of his work and its result rests mainly upon Him and his words. We shall give Him his place as Teacher and from Him learn the Truth that He is. His teachings have the personal character of which I have already said so much. They are the expression of his thought, but more than that, of Himself, and his interest in them is original and strong. Every parable that He gave to the people was of greater concern to Him than to them. They might disregard his words, but to Him they were full of feeling. The Kingdom which He described was his own Kingdom. Yet He valued it for this less than for the benefits it would have for those whose happiness was of more account than his own. The Father would be pleased and men would be pleased and men would be blessed, and no desire of his was to be in comparison with this.

I have spoken of the profound significance which He gave to "My." We know how much the word means to us. My country, my friend, my child, — the chief value is in the two letters which stand for myself. We blend our separate interests, and say "our," "ourselves," and we have the society with whose well-being our own is involved. One of the most suggestive sentences in the New Testament is in the Good Shepherd's words, spoken of Himself, and containing his whole heart, — "Rejoice with me, for I have found my sheep which was lost. I say unto you that even so there shall be joy in heaven." Even so, as the joy of the Shepherd who has found his sheep; the one, not the ninety and nine.

We miss the meaning of his words and the deeds which attended them if we do not see how much they meant to Him; that they were not things said and done in fulfilment of a mission, but were his own life, with its passion and desire. This was more evident at some times than at others. There was a day when the house in which He was most at home was darkened by death. He came at the call of his friends, and as He stood with them his sorrow was too great for control. He was troubled in spirit and He wept; not because this man only was dead, but because all men were dying and dead. The great soul sought the relief which nature gives. The Jews said, "Behold, how He loved him." They had no conception of the love which then held all sorrowing hearts in its compassion, and kept their sorrow for his own. He said in words which are simply like Himself, "Come unto Me, and I will give you rest." One may be pardoned for thinking of the young Buddha, and remembering how tenderly the way was prepared for him when he would walk abroad. No cripple should show himself out of doors lest the prince be grieved. No fallen leaf should remain upon the ground; there should be no hint of pain and death. "Come unto Me all ye that labor and are heavy laden." The rest He gave was his own. He went without it that He might bestow it. I suppose if we were all asked what is the deepest and strongest teaching He gave to weary, suffering men, we should answer, "The parable of the prodigal son." The name is of our making, not his. Rutherford called it "The forlorn son." Both names are true. I think it might well be called "The recovered son." But whatever name best pleases us, the parable itself expresses on the Father's side the feeling of Him who taught it. Over the wandering He sorrowed in great sadness. The affliction in a far country lay upon his heart. He waited and watched for the return. Nay, He did not tell it all. He went down where the boy was, and entreated him, and brought him home, and gave to him the ring and the shoes, and another chance to live. Every line is full of his feeling. This is his life. He seeks and He saves. Not one only, but all wanderers, all prodigals, He takes upon his heart, and He clothes them at his own cost, with the best robe, for He has no other. Every prodigal is called and shall be welcomed. His arms are strong enough, his heart is large enough, to hold every one of them. He is willing to be lifted up from the earth, if He may draw all men to Himself. The reason of his delight is in Himself, and it speaks in the same two letters — "This my son."

In all his life Christ is the reality. He does not declare it or represent it. He is the real. He is divine wisdom and love. We have the verities when we have Him. They show themselves, not becoming, but coming where they can be known of men. They are substantial and permanent. They are not handled, although the forms they assume may be touched. Christ was continually presenting the reality, and letting it be seen in contrast with that which had borne the name. One day men spoke to Him of the manna, and called it bread from heaven. He replied that was not real bread. It seemed so to your fathers, but bread itself is very different from that. "My Father giveth you the true bread from heaven. I am the bread of life." It is as if He had said, "The manna is an imitation." Again He spoke of the vine. Vines were to be seen everywhere;

possibly they ran over the window of the room where He was, or climbed beside the outer door. These are not real, He said, they are illustrations; they are like the carvings on the wall and about the pillars. "I am the true vine." The purpose of a vine He alone could fulfil. The grapes men plucked might indeed be refreshing. But He would give the true refreshment which the souls of men could receive. The sun was in the heavens, but He was the true light. "I am the Truth," He said. He was "full of grace and truth." "Grace and truth came" by Him. But there was more than this. He was more than true, even "the Truth." He said that He did not know the day or the hour when the Son of Man should come. That was a matter of knowledge which here He did not need to have. But the coming itself, the truth within the time, He knew. He said, "I will come again." "Heaven and earth shall pass away, but my word shall not pass away." The distinction between teaching the truth and being the Truth is not one of words. He meant to assert the completeness of his being, its sufficiency, its finality. It was not a representation, but that which other things represented. He would have approved the words written long afterward by one of his friends, "The things which are seen are temporal; but the things which are not seen are eternal." Truth is spiritual. The true things are everlasting. It is only when we keep this in mind that we understand Him. The truth which God is stands in Him, that it may do the work of God. It does not throw off a portion of itself and give this a man's form, and name. It reveals itself, and there is no break between the truth here and that which is beyond our sight. It has been well said that "you cannot draw a fence through the great ocean of infinity." You cannot divide the truth. We may attempt this by our definitions, but it must always fail. We are fortunate if we are not drowned in the effort to set the posts! Truth is one and eternal! "I am the Truth," He said.

His life becomes simple when we receive his own account of Himself, and see that He is controlled by the life which He is. "I am the Life," He said. "I give eternal life." There is but one life. It took his Personality with it, and around it, so far as this was possible. He lived therefore in two worlds; or, rather, He lived in both parts of the one world, in the seen and the unseen. There is no line between them in his thought. He lived among men, sat at their table, sailed in their boat, rested in their tomb. He talked with men, blessed their children, filled their nets. This was evident and actual. Yet He told them this: "The Son can do nothing of Himself, but what He seeth the Father doing; for what things soever He doeth, these the Son also doeth in like manner." If once we can receive such words as these, and not be offended in them, we shall know that here is the presence of the Truth which is recalling and regaining the world.

How very simple the works of Christ become in the presence of his reality! The most striking of them we call miracles, which is a poor and misleading name. They are described as "signs," and this suggests their character. They were works performed for the profit of men. But they did more than secure the immediate advantage, for they bore witness to the power which wrought them and was not exhausted. As they are often regarded, they lack the true element, for the power does not begin nor the result end as we suppose. Each sign comes out of the past and is the beginning of a series of benefits to be given and received. In each one He strives to get such hold upon a man that He can help him thoroughly, and in any world, and forever. He could always do more and greater things. The works bear the marks of self-restraint. Why was there any pause? They were entirely natural to Him, because He was in no wise limited by the regulations of the world. He was spirit and life, and things and forces must consent to his control. Physical nature was under the power of the Spirit. It had been so in the creation and always afterward. It was of importance then, as it is to-day, that this should be asserted. Men needed to know their independence of the world. They needed to see about them, and to feel within them, a power greater than that which prevailed in the course of nature. Even if they were obliged for a time to submit to the forces around them, it was well to feel that they might become free. Men had been known to worship the forms and powers of nature. It resulted in evil. The best way to break up this custom was to show the subjection of these divinities of the air and the sea. Here was one who could govern them, and He spoke in the name of God. It was an advance for men to find themselves greater than their divinities, because they were spirit. This had been said before, but Christ told it again, and repeatedly, and in many ways, that men might see the greater power, and seeing it in Him find it in themselves. Because He belonged to both worlds, especially to the world of the Spirit, all his works were simple, and readily performed. They were signs of his own nature. They were samples, specimens, of the real work which He was to do. They were his assurance of a time when there would be no men blind, or lame, or dead. If the small acts convinced them of his truth they could trust Him for the more important works which were needed, which should entirely deliver men from the world and the flesh into the liberty of the sons of God. The words of the Gospel are thorough and vigorous. "As many as received Him, to them gave He the right to become children of God, even to them that believe on his name; which were born, not of blood, nor of the will of the flesh, nor of the will of man, but of God." This was to be here. The two worlds were together, the world of the seen and of the unseen; or, in terms which were afterward familiar, the world of nature and of grace.

A miracle comes from the influence of the spiritual world, when it is brought to bear upon the world of things. It has been said that it "stands for the mystery of human existence," and is "the symbol of the preëminence of spirit over nature." Christ would have preferred to have men know Him without these signs; for spiritual discernment was higher. Yet it is doubtful if they could have known Him but for such works as arrested their attention, and made them believe that He was from God. They believed because of the things they saw, though these were of less account than his own Truth. "Believe Me that I am in the Father, and the Father in Me; or else believe Me for the very works' sake." The miracles were on a lower plane of evidence than the Truth to which they gave witness, but they were effective. How much higher our Lord rated his work upon the spirit is shown in a very striking way in the startling assurance He gave on his last night — "He that believeth on Me, the works that I do shall he do also; and greater works than these shall he do." He meant that to open the eyes of a man so that he should see his father was less than to give him the vision of God; that to enable a man to walk the streets was less than to persuade him to walk with God; that even to raise one from the dead was less than bringing a man into the eternal life of the Spirit. So far from encouraging men to wonder at his power in the world, He taught that they should do works of surpassing value.

He required faith. This was not needed for a common miracle. But common miracles He did not care to work, unless by means of them He could find the soul and make it whole. This needed the soul's consent, and this was faith. He was not here to be admired, but to be known. He did not care to give a benefit which could be acquired in some other way, and would come to an end. Every work of mercy was, in his intent, the seed of another, and this process was to be endless. I think that we make less account of Christ's miracles than has been made at other times. The attention has been more upon Him and the truths which He taught. Still, we ought to regard his works carefully; not with a view to their repetition, but as the disclosure of his spiritual place and dominion. We could prove his acts by surpassing them. Those who have done the "greater works" of which He spoke appear to have no trouble with the miracles of the New Testament. Perhaps confidence in ourselves would have been fairer than our doubt of Him. Many are the wonderful works which are mentioned, though not all are told, and they are in entire keeping with his words. They were so numerous that it was thought needless to make the record of them. Thirty years afterward they stood before the memory of men who saw them like a forest of trees one cannot think of counting. The latest of the writers went so far as to say that if all the things which Jesus had done should be written, he supposed that the world itself would not contain the books. Reading the memoirs as one reads any book, it is more than difficult to regard these unnumbered signs as the invention of such men as were his friends, and gave their life to Him whom they knew as Truth; who told what they saw and heard, as one of them said, that others might have fellowship with them. Such signs need very clear evidence, and we should question the witnesses, their truthfulness and intelligence. This is the part of prudence. But when all the testimony is given which the nature of the case makes possible, and when the evidence is sure enough to be accepted in regard to events less unusual, something better than denial, or incredulity, may fairly be asked of us. We have come to believe too many things which at first seemed beyond belief to be hastily turned from anything which brings to us reasonable credentials. There have been too many surprises in our time to warrant a careless unbelief. The scientific method and spirit are alone proper. Look, question, decide, search, find, determine. To settle it beforehand with ourselves that certain things cannot be done is not the road to knowledge. The time for that conceit has gone by. The unusual is not of necessity the difficult. The quality of a miracle is in its strangeness, not in the force which it needs. It requires no more of wisdom or skill than a hundred things to which we are accustomed. If it needs our effort to believe, it should need effort to rule the miracle out of the works of God. It is hard to believe, when one thinks upon it, that the Almighty has done his last work, and that thenceforth all is repetition; that the world, and the universe, are but a mechanism, which is to pursue only its unvarying round. Who shall say that God has thus mortgaged Himself to his past, and denied Himself the pleasure of doing a new thing, of using a new method, of meeting any event of life in any way which He chooses? To deny the possibility of a miracle is strangely to limit the Almighty. We talk of the laws of nature as if they were statutes. Nature does not legislate. What we thus name laws are but the Creator's methods, and these are forces, not fetters. Be very sure that when the Maker of heaven and earth wishes to work in a new way He will do it. It is at great times, at some eventful point, that history has the record of such variation from his custom. The creation was new. Strange works attended the delivery of Israel from Egypt. They marked the coming of the Lord and the coming of his Kingdom. They were not more grand or more divine than the events they stood among.

I have lingered upon the works of Christ longer than I intended. I leave them as a part of the fourfold record of his life. The story is simply told, as if the writers had long since ceased to be surprised by them. In the thirty years which preceded the writing they had come to know Him better, and their increased knowledge shows itself in their steadiness of mind and their assured confidence. Long and full of events were the years between the day when St. John took the mother of Jesus to his home, and the day when as an old man he wrote out his remembrance of One who loved him. Time may have had something to do with the quietness and naturalness of the narrations of the three years which Jesus spent among men, going about doing good.

The works are incidents in the life. They belong in a life which moves with even flow from the beginning. Let them be judged in their place, and with the company they keep; by the reason for them and the result from them. The works confirm his authority and establish his teaching. They are the signs of larger gifts.

Before we leave this simple account of the life of Christ it is necessary that we dwell for a moment upon two facts which have a place of importance in his teaching. The first is prayer. It is true that this did not begin with Him. It is embodied in the entire system of religion which is taught in the Bible. He found it. He learned it in his home at Nazareth. He taught his disciples to find comfort and strength in it. There were times when He spent a whole night in prayer. It is clear that He depended upon it. It is equally clear that He expected his apostles to depend upon it. He would not have made them his messengers save as He knew that they would pray, and in prayer obtain the grace and light they needed. But what was prayer as He taught it? It was a spiritual act. It was the intercourse of the soul with God. There was asking, but there was much more. There was the being consciously in the presence of God. The voice presents requests; but there is more than requests. If I may quote my own words, "The better part of prayer is not the asking, but the kneeling where we can ask, the resting there, the stopping there, drawing out the willing moments in heavenly communion with God, within the closet, with the night changed into the brightness of the day by the light of Him who all the night was in prayer to God." Surely, the soul would have strength which should thus wait at the source of strength.

Requests are made and answered; sometimes as we wish, and sometimes with changes and delays. But there is no delay in blessing the soul which, at leisure from itself, waits with God; and He knew that with it men could be trusted to do all which He would have them do. This is an essential part of his teaching, and cannot be taken from the truth and duty which He gave.

> More things are wrought by prayer
> Than this world dreams of; for what were men,
> If, knowing God, they lift not hands of prayer
> Both for themselves and those who call them friend?
> For so the whole round earth is every way
> Bound by gold chains about the feet of God.

The second fact to which allusion was made is the Sabbath. This also did not begin with Him. It is conspicuous in the religious life of his people, from a time before the giving of the Law on Siani. He found the day, and kept it holy when a boy in Nazareth, and in the years which brought Him on to manhood. When He began his teaching the day which was made for man had become oppressive. The rules and customs which had gathered about it would have seemed ludicrous had they not been so heavy a burden at a time which was meant for gladness. He did not abolish the day, or release men from a sacred regard for it. But He set the day free. He delivered it, and restored it to its own meaning. In all this He made it plain that He did not intend to do away with the Sabbath. A man does not restore a building which he intends in a few days to destroy. The changes which Christ wrought are a witness to his purpose to have the day kept after its original design. Under the direction of his apostles the first day of the week took the place of the seventh, and was the day of sacred delight, the "sweet day of rest," the weekly Easter with its celebration of the Resurrection of Christ. It may be regarded, then, as having a fixed place in the teaching of Christ. It is to be a day of rejoicing. We are released from work; we are set free from the round of daily duties, that the soul may have its opportunity, and that we may quietly foster and enjoy our faith and love in worship, in meditation, in communion, in all which makes us more spiritual, more Divine. This is Christ's intent. It is obvious that the more nearly we can keep the day according to his desire the richer its hours will be; the closer our walk with God, the firmer our purpose to be like Him; the more nearly perfect our peace and joy, the sanctity of our spirit, the divinity of our life.

It was in the knowledge of Himself as the Truth, as belonging in two worlds, that we have the explanation of his life. It is in this that its peculiar value consists. It is vain to compare Him with others who have lived, and to find resemblances to his teachings and his works. The more resemblances of this kind which we can discover the better is it for the world. But He stands alone, in his own consciousness, and in his constant teaching, and in the purpose of his life as He declared it. He alone lives as the embodiment of the love which God is. His first relation is with God, and this is never changed. Keeping this, He comes really into the world, that the love which He is may become life for men. It is thus that He teaches and helps; thus that he gives his life — "I have power to lay it down, and I have power to take it again." It is thus that He claims all sheep, all sinners, as his own, and seeks them that He may save them; thus that He goes into the far country that He may bring home the prodigal, his own prodigal. All this God would do. It belongs in our idea of God. It is in his Son that He does it. The great desire, full of pity and love, the great longing for his own; the Divine goodness and grace which encircle the earth and sweep through the ages; the almightiness which is informed with compassion, and cannot rest, but will have its own, — all the heart of God finds men where they are, and is faithful to love, mighty to save. "He will abundantly pardon." But the heart of God among men bears the name which was given by the angel — "Jesus;" and the other, which is "God with us." We are out of the range of philosophy. This is Truth. He does not simply reveal God. He is really the Love of God.

Of course the world did not receive Him. He was despised and rejected by those who saw only their own disappointment in Him. At last He was crucified. But He said repeatedly that He should not be holden of death. He was the stronger. On the third day He appeared among men. They saw Him and knew that it was He. Many saw Him. The faith which had been rudely shaken was quickly restored. For a few weeks He remained among his friends, then He returned into the skies. The account is given with brevity and simplicity. Upon the fact of the Resurrection his disciples rested their lives and based their ministry. They lived in the knowledge of it, and many sealed their devotion with their lives. To the closing events of Christ's life his disciples attached the chief significance. These stand highest in their thought. They preached them as the centre and heart of their message to the world. It is evident that there was a profound meaning in the death of the Truth and the Life. I know that Life and Truth cannot die. But the body in which they lived could die. For Him, then, to consent to be obedient to death, when He could have avoided it easily, was a fact before which it becomes us to be still. It is clear from his own teaching that He intended to find his sheep and his sons by the way of the cross. This He has done. This was the understanding of the apostles, and by this rule they ordered their ministry, and gained the world for Him. As often as we contemplate the close of his life, let us find the meaning of it in Himself; not in the cross, but in the Truth which uses it.

I am the Truth, He said.

V

THE CAUSE OF CHRIST IN THE HANDS OF MEN

THE CAUSE OF CHRIST IN THE HANDS OF MEN

I HAVE written at length of the Person in whom the Creator and Father of men seeks to recall them to their true life; to give them again of his own life. Has his purpose been accomplished? As we advance, and see Him in the world and mark his influence, is it clear that the Divine thought is being fulfilled? While his work is not completed at any point, it has gone far enough for an intelligent opinion of its merit and promise. It is not possible to see all that He has done, because much of it is in the hearts of men, in their character, their motives and intentions, their inclinations and affections, and the disclosure of these is imperfect. We know what He has done for us, and in some measure what He has done for others. With the necessary limitation of our knowledge, there is abundant and conclusive evidence regarding the effect of Christianity upon men; upon society and its institutions; upon literature, science, art; upon the home and the school; upon the woman and the child; upon charity and all the virtues; upon life, liberty, and the pursuit of happiness. In tracing the course of his life upon the earth we are to keep always in mind the Personality of Christ. It was this which He gave to the world — Himself. "I am" stands before his teaching and the works which attended it. He was in the gifts which He bestowed. Buddhism could live without Buddha. Christianity is impossible without Christ. He is the breath, the soul, the life, of the truth. He is the Love which loves men into love.

The men whom He called to be disciples and then Apostles were held to Him by personal devotion. The readiness with which they left all to follow Him is a witness to the power which was his. He had nothing to offer them of earthly reward; He insisted upon their humility; He told them that they could not be his disciples unless they denied themselves, and took up their cross; He spoke to them of his own death, and of the tribulation they would have in the world; at last He gave Himself to the cross, and died, and was entombed. But they were not moved from Him, save one, who in a "desperate self-respect" fled from the world where there seemed to be no place for him. Confused they were, the eleven men who were the disciples; disappointed, desolate, stricken; but they kept their faith in Him and waited for that which was to come. What held them? The Love which drew them. It was a wonderful power which Christ had. I do not call it supernatural, for it was of Himself. He called them and there was power in his words. The voice, the look, the whole presence, drew them to Him. They were not poor men, weak men; but men well-to-do, substantial citizens of the North country, who proved afterward that they could teach their own people and the world; and their word has gone out into all the earth. Nothing in our libraries is so precious as their writings. They could bear all things, even to martyrdom, and die in exultation, and leave their names for adoration. It was the perfect Love which called them; the Love which is the strongest, Divinest thing known in heaven, and which was incarnate in Him. It attracted, persuaded, compelled, the men whose hearts it reached, whose love could recognize the eternal Love and be taken into it and held there, so that the power of the Divine Love should be around them, keeping and guiding; inspiring them for the life of love which was to follow his, and be his and theirs. If I knew what the perfect Love is I could better tell how it found these hearts which

Love had made, and pleased itself and them. Were they not of one nature with Him who came to their boats, and filled their nets, and made them fishers of men? They loved because they were first loved. The Love of Christ constrained them. It made them the men whom Christ needed, whom the Love of God needed, for a ministry which must begin and end in love. We like the answer of these men to the call of Christ. It was so hearty, and simple, and trusting; not hindered by question, or despoiled by delay. "And He called them. And they immediately left the ship and their father, and followed Him." It was great confidence in Him. But this is not more to be admired than his confidence in them.

Let us think of the meaning of his life; of the magnificent purpose and expectation in which He was to give his life, to be lifted up that He might draw all men to Himself. Yet after his crucifixion He went no more among strangers, and soon He returned to heaven. Who were to take up his ministry and carry it through the lands which had not heard his name? These men, who for a few months had walked with Him and learned of Him, — by these his word and work were to be preserved and extended till every man should hear of Him. They knew Him, and they were ready to do anything at his bidding.

He knew them and He trusted all to them. I think this is the largest instance of faith in the history of the world. If they failed Him, his cause was at an end. The cross would be the headstone at its grave. He knew they would not fail Him, for his love held their hearts. I think of Nelson's signal as the battle of Trafalgar was to begin — "England confides that every man will do his duty." — "I have no signal for confides," the officer said. "May I not say expects?" Nelson consented, but his own word was the better, with more heart in it, — "England confides." The words express as well as words can, fittingly, beautifully, the thought of Christ when his hour had come. He confided that every man would do his duty. Every man did. It is a testimony to them, but even more to Him. It was well written by one who joined them — "The greatest is love."

After his resurrection, and a little time before his withdrawal from these disciples, Christ met seven of them by the sea of Galilee, where He helped them fill the nets which all the night had been spread in vain, and gave them a lesson in trust which could not be forgotten. When He had given them to eat of fish which had not been brought in their net, — the one hundred and fifty-fourth, — He asked one of the little group, who had been in some degree a leader among them, if he loved Him. Three times He asked. He was asking all the men through one. It was the question of the future. Everything depended upon the answer. There was nothing to hold them but Love, their love living in his. The reply contented Him, and He ordained them to the care of his sheep and lambs; for He was the Good Shepherd, and a shepherd King, as his ancestor had been. After this He was with them in Jerusalem where He bade them wait till they should receive power; for they were to be witnesses to Him "in Jerusalem, and in all Judea, and in Samaria, and unto the uttermost part of the earth." It was a confidence in the truth, and in these men whom He loved, which was like Himself. At last He led them to the mount called Olivet, and from there ascended to the glory which He had before the world was. The end was in keeping with the beginning.

The friends returned to the city, as they had been told to do. They were but few in number, and were unnoticed. They would have been oppressed with a strange loneliness but for the assurance that He would be with them still. He would be close enough to help them, while they would be allowed a true liberty. They had the promise of the Holy Spirit whom He would send.

They waited by themselves, living over the three years of their discipleship, and the last days of sadness and triumph. In an upper room, where their home was for a time, they turned their minds heavenward and prayed for the power from above. They needed it. There were a few who shared their hope, and among these was "Mary, the mother of Jesus," "blessed among women." Think on the course of the world since that time! Has there ever been gathered council or congress which, for dignity and solemnity, could compare with that? They waited. It was like a ship with her sails set, watching for the breeze. The world was waiting for the coming power, though it knew it not. It was waiting for those unregarded men — men of faith, with a history; men firm by nature and training; holding to the ancestral belief and hope; members of a religious nation. They had not been asked to change their faith, and they were not to ask their countrymen. Judaism had not produced Christianity, but it was fulfilled in it. The Gentile religions, which were as little able to produce the new faith as thistles to bear figs, were to part with all which was untrue and to receive the Truth which was from heaven. Christ was Himself, and there was no one before Him who was like Him, as there has been no one after Him. These Jews who had become Christians were to announce that the Messiah had come. He was not the desire of the world, but He was infinitely more. This was to be said everywhere, beginning at Jerusalem where He had been crucified. The Truth must go forth from the Cross. Out from that narrow door which was not far from Calvary was to issue the Love of God, to seek and find its own. The Kingdom of heaven was in that upper room, waiting. The disciples were indeed in the presence of the King, who had called them friends. They had no chief, save as strength of character asserted itself. They were not organized, save as a globe stands about its centre. They had no forms, but the form of spirit and of truth. The precepts of their Teacher were their laws, and these could never lose control. They had Christ, and his Love held their love, and what God had joined together could not be put asunder.

Their time came. For designation it is called the Day of Pentecost, the time of the first fruits, and the name was well chosen; but Pentecost had come a thousand times before, and this day alone is remembered. Strange things were seen and heard in Jerusalem. The promised power descended upon the disciples and those who were with them. It was a spiritual power, giving vigor to their minds and hearts, and enabling them to speak with a wisdom and force which made their words effective among the listeners. This was entirely simple, for it was the gift of the Spirit who is God to the kindred spirit who is man. In this power the disciples preached. The result was that many, being persuaded and enabled by the Spirit, believed the Word which was preached; three thousand in one day, and others afterward. It was the first attempt of Christianity to get into the world and become its life, and it was signally successful. This was well called "Power from on high." Under its influence "the Lord added to them day by day those that were saved" — for this was the designation given them. It was in this form of the Holy Spirit that Christ was henceforth to be with his disciples. It was expedient that Jesus of Nazareth should go away. There was need of a presence more widely diffused, in all places at all times, which could readily enter the spirit of man and abide there, and direct his thoughts and enlarge his life. They had now the completion of the baptismal creed and confession — the Father, the Son, and the Holy Ghost. The order is plainly declared in the New Testament. First the eternal Father whom no man hath seen; then the Son in whom God is revealed to men; then the Holy

Spirit in whom the Son is revealed to the world; and there is one God. I do not enter upon the theological bearing of these truths. The mission of the Holy Spirit is definitely set forth. It connects itself immediately with the work of Christ, and so with the Love of the Father. It is necessary at this point that the words of Christ concerning the Holy Spirit should be carefully marked — "When the Comforter is come, whom I will send unto you from the Father, even the Spirit of truth, which proceedeth from the Father, He shall bear witness of Me." "He shall guide you into all the truth." "He shall glorify Me, for He shall take of Mine, and shall declare it unto you." "He shall teach you all things, and bring to your remembrance all that I said unto you." It is evident, therefore, that this Divine Presence is to carry forward the Love of the Father and the mission of Christ in which that Love is fulfilled. The Holy Spirit is to be in men, the presence of God, the Love of the Son of God, quickening and renewing their hearts, creating them anew with a new life. Hence we have the strong words of the chief Apostle: "As many as are led by the Spirit of God, these are sons of God." This is the day of the Holy Spirit.

Thus at Pentecost men received life. They

came fully under the first Commandment, and under the second, for every man's need became another's opportunity. There was a quick test. None lacked, for none owned. Many tongues were heard, but they spoke in the one language of brotherhood.

The new gift went farther. It was to be helpful at once. One of the Apostles, who had come to the knowledge of his power in preaching, attempted his first independent sign, that which we ineffectively call a miracle. Some experience had been granted him before, in an apprentice way, but he was now to work by himself. A man lame from his birth lay at the Beautiful Gate of the Temple, and he looked, as his wont was, upon this disciple and another Galilean, that he might receive alms. The Apostle seized and held him with his eyes, raising the confidence which he was to disappoint. "I have no silver and gold," he said, "but I will give you what I have." This was one of the marks of the new faith. Its ministers made no pretence and offered no excuse. What they did not have was of no use to them or to the world. Taking the cripple by the hand, he lifted him, and for the first time the man stood upon his feet. The surgeon who reported the case said that his feet and ankle-bones received strength. Things looked well for the new cause.

One thing was wanting, and that was soon supplied, when Herod slew an Apostle with a sword, and proposed to send another to the same fate. Earlier than this, a man who had been called to office in the society was stoned for his boldness in the faith. The cause was now well on its way. Could it continue? As long as those who believed in it remained true.

But it had the world to gain. The world knew nothing of it; or, knowing, was hostile to it. The Jews had not swerved from their opposition, neither the leaders nor the people. Persecution grew more severe. In this is a sign of the force in the new faith. Strange that all the authority which remained to the nation was turned against the carpenter's son! The Nazarene had made Himself feared in high places, and He had not lifted a hand, and only one of his followers had drawn a sword. Here was a growing influence which could not be reasoned down, and thus far there had been no force which could resist it. Observe its vitality and the method of it, and think what this signifies. It was a notable event when from its enemies came its stoutest friend. He was not of Jerusalem, which was in his favor. Galilee gave the first Apostles. This man came even farther. The comparative largeness of provincial life was on his side. He had grown up among men. He was a Roman, and this gave him position and daring. He was religious, and his religion was a reality. He was a Jew, and loving his people he sprang to the defence of the poor remnant of their liberty. Fearless, determined, aggressive, he found his passion enlarged as he saw a good man stoned, who died in triumph under the open heaven. He kept the clothes of the murderers, and when they resumed them he took up their work. He could do nothing in a small way. He was mad exceedingly, and he thought the cause justified his violence. It is some witness to the strength of the Nazarene, as He was described, that He made Saul of Tarsus angry through his whole being. His madness is as good as a day's miracles, for evidence. The conversion of the High Priest would have meant less. He consented to be taught, and to be enrolled as a disciple. The name he had hated became at once his glory. He waited that he might find himself. He meditated in Arabia where only God could teach him. He learned from those who had walked with the Master of his life and his word. He confirmed his faith, we may suppose, by visiting the places where the Lord had suffered and died. He promptly and publicly declared himself a believer in the risen Lord, and then abandoning his profession went forth to be the preacher.

The more he taught the more he believed. As there is nothing succeeds like success, so there is nothing believes like belief. A zeal for Christ possessed him, greater even than his madness had been. He cared for nothing beside. He was absorbed in his devotion. His feeling was long afterward expressed by his Moravian friend: "I have one passion, and it is He, He only." He went to his own people. He went beyond them to the excluded nations. The door for this was opened by a Divine hand when the word was carried by another Apostle to a Roman soldier at Cesarea who had commended himself by his prayers and gifts. Then the work spread. Men believed wherever they heard. They were called and called out, and by this word were known. We have translated it, which is a pity. The faith was taking on more of form. The adjective which had described the Teacher became a proper name, and those who belonged to Him were called after it, not by any appointment, but for convenience. They were called Christians as their Master was Christ. The name given by others grew in favor. The Apostles went through their own land and beyond it. St. Paul went far abroad, carrying the Good News of God, as the Word came to be described. Churches were formed of Jews and Gentiles, and were fostered with apostolic care. St. Paul visited them in repeated journeys, and when absent wrote to them. His letters make a large and important part of the early and the later Christian literature. They were letters, not doctrinal treatises. They established no schedule of belief, after the manner of later times. He taught doctrine, indeed, but not a system. All his letters enforced the Christian teaching. He wrote one letter which is in the largest sense theological, and which is a strong statement of his belief. This was to a church which he had not visited, which needed a formal statement of the Christian faith that should serve as a constitution at Rome, and wherever the new church at Rome had influence. This letter by no means contents itself with belief, but makes conduct of essential importance. In his letters St. Paul stated in his own terms that which he had learned, with confirmation out of philosophy, and history, and experience. He added nothing to the teaching of the Master. He did not teach by parable, but in a more immediate and direct manner. That he gave form to the teaching of Christ is evident; but they are mistaken who think he altered the teaching itself. He expanded the central teaching of Christ, that He had come to seek and to save that which was lost; and he defined the loss, and the seeking, and the saving. He taught in what way and for what reasons the Good Shepherd gave his life for the sheep. He declared the resurrection of the dead in words which remain the clearest exposition of Immortality. He exalted love and enforced it in the finest sentences ever written concerning it. One phrase has become in our time almost a definition. Not content with such themes, he guided the churches in their affairs, and in the behavior of their members. There was need of this, for many had brought the vices of their old religion into the new faith. They needed rebuke, warning, entreaty, if any good was to come to them under their new name, and it was to be commended by their lives. The best proof of Christianity must be the lives of those whom it controls. It must show its power to save by saving, its ability to create by creating. The teacher of this faith can never attach too much importance to the conduct of those who hold it. This is not a large fraction of life: it is the whole. The act of the will is as real as the act of the hand. This is not to be forced for the sake of evidence; but the religion is to be unhindered and obeyed. Let it show what it can do. Some of the things about which the Apostle wrote may seem small for a man to be concerned with who more than any other had the Kingdom of

God in his charge. But it is the peculiarity of
the Kingdom of God, that it concerns itself with
small things, with unimportant men, and with the
actions which are their character. It is a mark
of Christianity that it makes the man of large
moment, and if the man then his conduct. Let
us remember the words of the herald of the Kingdom: " He that hath two coats, let him impart to
him that hath none; and he that hath food, let
him do likewise." " Extort no more than that
which is appointed you." There is a majesty in
St. Paul's great pages; but I mark also the divinity of his small sentences whereby he seeks to
persuade men to live in truth, and purity, and
charity. He had learned the mind of Christ.
This was his claim for himself, and he had need to
assert it, for his right to preach was not unchallenged. That he had learned some things of St.
Peter, and James the Lord's brother, he declared.
But with all the force at his command he asserted
that the Gospel which he had preached he had
not learned of man, but had received it " by
the revelation of Jesus Christ." It was this
which made the tremendous energy of his life, and
made him one of the two or three most influential
men whom the world has known. The facts of
the new faith, the incidents in Christ's life, the
teaching which He gave, could be readily learned

from his friends. It was quite as simple that the spirit of this should be given into his spirit by the Spirit of truth to which it was akin; that the meaning should be thus bestowed, and direction for the employment of the teaching, the right adjustment of it within itself and in the minds of men, and all which we mean by inspiration, which is entirely simple when one knows that he too is spirit. This did not teach him everything, but it did furnish him generously and truly for the work, the large work, which he was to do. It left him a free man, even under the teaching of the Spirit of God. Every one who prays for guidance prays for inspiration. When the reality of this is perceived, its extent offers no difficulty. Here was St. Paul's authority with himself and the world. He had not grown into the Christian faith. He had been stopped on his way, and with his consent, which was promptly given, had been taken up into the Way — for by this name the new faith was soon called. This was the place, this was the time, from which Christianity was reaching out on its mission. Let it be noted that Christ was directing it still. The assertion of this abounds in the records.

We must not fail to ask what Christianity was at that time. What did St. Paul and the others teach? They repeated the teaching of Christ in addresses and in letters. The Apostles did more than recite his words. They preached Christ Himself. They did not merely commend Him to the admiration of men, or his teaching to their belief. They preached Him. They did not teach a system of Christian philosophy, or present a scheme of Christian conduct. Everything was to be practical and thorough. Christ did not come to set an example in Himself, nor to give to the world a series of patterns. Examples are very well in their way, but not interesting, and not very effective. In giving life He provided for conduct, and He sent men out to live and give life. They did not talk about Him, they presented Him. They sought to bring men under his control. They knew that if men consented to this, He would cleanse their hearts, inform their minds, direct their lives. They sought to unite each man to Him, vitally, spiritually, for wisdom and life. It was personal on both sides. Christ and the man were to be joined as vine and branch.

We can come nearer. While they presented Christ, the Person, they laid the chief stress on the close of his life. This held the force of all which was before it, yet this stood out by itself in their minds. St. Paul said, " We preach Christ crucified." His resurrection completed the work of the Cross. But it was the Cross to which they drew the minds of men; to Christ, who by means of the Cross, in a special manner and degree, gave his life for the world. It was in this form that the life of Christ passed out among the nations. It is not likely that Constantine saw the Cross in the sky. But the early Apostles of Christianity saw it always before their minds, and by this sign they thought to conquer the world. The truths preached by the Apostles and believed by the first Christians are believed and preached to-day. The Christian minister of last Sunday, if he had missed his way to his own door, and had found himself in one of those early assemblies of disciples, which had prolonged its meeting, would probably have left his sermon in its case, but could have talked with them on equal terms, gaining from them something of vividness, and giving to them something of experience, but concurring with them on all the truths which are essential to a Christian life. I wish I might have been that erring minister!

Was the world prepared to receive this new teaching? It needed it. The religions which had held the ground had lost their force, certainly in the lands around Palestine which would first be reached. Think as well of these as you will. It cannot be very well, and their time was over. There was no reason why they should linger. The characters which had been fashioned under the ancient faiths were not often to be admired. At last not even the gods could have been respected by high-minded men. The language of one of our American scholars is to the point when he writes of the elder Cato, that he possessed almost every virtue not specially blessed by Christ, but that there was not one of the Beatitudes of Christ in which he, the best of the Romans, could have claimed a part; and that there are none of the Roman divinities who possessed any of these virtues. To come down a hundred years, even Marcus Aurelius, philosopher and saint, who has reached renown as one of the best men those times can present, and because of whom we are bidden admire the times in which he was possible, "obtained the apotheosis of his profligate wife and of his dissolute colleague, building temples for their worship, instituting priesthoods in their names, and in all respects yielding them divine honors." It is not strange that Christianity suffered under his rule. This has been termed "a tragical fact." If his religion was to keep its place, there was no room for the new faith of Judea. But the need was there. "I apprehend," said Vespasian, as death came close to him, — "I apprehend that I am going to be a god." Was the way then open for the Son of God? To find the people ready to throw off the forms which remained, and to accept another faith, coming from a Jewish province, and one whose history, so far as it was known, had little to commend it, was more than prudent men, relying on their own judgment, were entitled to expect. It was a bold intent, to present a religion which forbade many things to which the people were accustomed, and which they held right and even essential; whose spirit was charity, in that age, and whose deeds were service; which made all men brethren, the children of one Father, who was the one God; which accounted it profitable to give up the world for the soul's sake, and to lay up in heaven that which had been earned upon the earth; which had no altars or images, and enjoined worship only in spirit and in truth; where priests would lose their office and become suppliants for mercy by the side of the king and the slave. Could the attempt succeed? The Athenian had graved upon one of his many altars, "To an unknown God." When St. Paul declared the Unknown, and in the same breath bore witness to the resurrection of his Master, the most courteous response he received was the promise to hear him at another time. If there was ever an apparently wild, desperate enterprise undertaken in the name of religion, it was in the purpose to establish through the Roman Empire the teaching of Christ and Him crucified. This was attempted. This was done.

It is not difficult to perceive the moral desolation of the period when Christianity first ventured abroad. Historians have not measured their words, and excess is easy. But there can be no doubt of the social and moral ruin which was everywhere to be found. In the words of Professor Jowett, "To see the world in its worst estate we turn to the age of the satirists and of Tacitus, when all the different streams of evil, coming from East, West, North, South, the vices of barbarism and the vices of civilization, remnants of ancient cults, and the latest refinements of luxury and impurity, met and commingled on the banks of the Tiber." I have said enough to those who know more. Of course there were good men and women. There were sincere worshippers. There were defenders of the faith, and even trials for heresy. Anaxagoras was "banished for suggesting that the god Helios was a mass of molten iron." There was religion which had control of certain lives. Indeed, the very word religion suggests a belief in unseen powers, and with this points of contact might be found. There may have been sincerity even in persecution, as there was when Saul of Tarsus was on the other side. The ethical standards were different from ours and lower than they have since become. Let all this be acknowledged, and the extreme difficulty of passing just judgment on the religion of another nation. We seldom do it on the religion of another man, even. Still, making all allowances, it was a very unpromising field for missionary effort. But upon it the young faith was to enter. The reasons of its triumph have been stated by Gibbon, and Merivale, and others, and are too familiar for repetition. There is not a little truth in their words. The forces they describe must have had their effect, but they were not sufficient for the results. Perhaps history did not feel warranted in going to the under-current of influence. History is always in danger of coming upon religion. Religion gets wonderfully involved with the affairs of men, and moves along in every advance. But it is quiet and unobtrusive. Writers sometimes overlook it. It was by virtue of the spirit which was in it, of the thought of God and the steady movement of his intention, that the Christian truth went forward to do what it had been appointed and foreordained to do.

The men who were to change the world had

little learning or position. They had seen their Master crucified, and had seen Him afterward living. With entire devotion to his service they went out with their spiritual weapons. They were tolerated as harmless till they came to be feared. Paganism desired them as allies, and was quickly refused. The force which sought to compel the alliance was cruel to no purpose. The messengers of the faith could not be conquered. The first witnesses died, but others entered into their work. They made converts among the common people, and gained some of higher rank. At length the Emperor extended his favor to the Christians, and they had the formal right to be. "The religion of the despised Nazarene, against the most savage and persistent resistance ever known in the world, had conquered the empire." It "had transformed the world's history." Paganism had by no means been removed, but Christianity had not been destroyed. That decreased, this increased. The statue on the Bosphorus with the head of Constantine and the form of Apollo, with a piece of the true cross, has been thought a fit image of the time — a heathen body with a Christian head, and Christian life at the heart. On his death-bed the Emperor sought baptism and said, "Now all ambiguity vanishes." Julian strove in vain to bring back the fallen divinities. The words put upon his lips may never have been spoken; but the Nazarene had conquered.

It is not for me here to trace the extension of this work, to which the name Missions has been given. It was, of course, inevitable that these should be carried on by men who saw their title to discipleship in the obedience of Christ who had bidden them go into all the world and preach the Gospel to the whole creation. There was only one thing to be done in the presence of their "marching orders." Within them was the very spirit of the Gospel, that is, Love. Love insisted on sharing every good with every neighbor. The greater the good the greater the duty. The great leader was not of the first company; but all the disciples, save one, were missionaries of the faith. Those of the multitude assembled at Pentecost whom the faith won to itself became missionaries as they returned to their scattered homes. The power of the truth was in it. Let it touch life, and it would make itself felt. The early successes were encouraging. It is not possible to determine their extent with accuracy. When all allowances are considered, it is clear that Christianity was acquiring strength and influence. The world could have been offered no other religion which could thus make itself regarded. Each new convert was a new witness, and converts multiplied. We find Pliny writing that around him men of every rank were turning to the new religion; in city and country the "superstition" made its way, and the temples were almost forsaken. The emperor replied to him that if the Christians refused to honor the gods they were to be punished, but that otherwise they were not to be interfered with. They did refuse homage to the gods, and they were ready, more than ready, to seal their testimony with their life. Strong men and gentle women died in triumph, by the forms of death which cruel ingenuity could devise. This helped where it was meant to hinder. They lived with their hearts upon the cross of Christ, and coveted the cross for themselves. Tertullian wrote to the persecutors: "All your refinements of cruelty can accomplish nothing: on the contrary, they do but serve to win men over to this sect. Our number increases the more you persecute us." Again, he asserts their right to live because of the truth they were teaching. "Every Christian mechanic has found God, and shows Him to you; and can teach you all in fact that you require to know of God; even though Plato says that it is hard to find out the Creator of the universe, and impossible, after one has found Him, to make Him known to all."

The conviction is to me unavoidable as I study

these events, that there was here the light and life which the world needed; and that they were offered by the Creator as his new and special gift. This is the meaning of it all. The new faith was doing an indispensable work which nothing else could attempt. There is much beauty and force in the saying of Augustine, "Christ appeared to the men of a decrepit and dying world, that, while all around them was decaying, they might through Him receive a new and youthful life." To this the German historian adds, "And the higher life which Christianity came to impart required no brilliant outward splendor for the manifestation of its glory."

In every direction the new faith was spreading. It usually reached the cities first, and there it was more likely to be received than among the ruder people of the country, whose language it would often be difficult for strangers to speak. With this diffusion of the Christian faith we are not now concerned. It is certain that this came out of Jerusalem, made its way through neighboring and distant lands, going farther and farther until it has gained recognition around the globe, and stands to-day wherever civilization flourishes, with commerce and the arts, with learning, liberty, opportunity. By its own force, that is, the Divine force embodied in it, it has quietly pursued its way, and now it holds the world, and holds the future.

But what has been the influence of Christianity? Let it be remembered that the work is very far from completion. Yet something can even now be required of it. Its advance is evident. But what has it done as it has moved on from the land which knew it first? I can readily give you a good answer, but I must give it in a book. Some fourteen or fifteen years ago a course of lectures was delivered before the Lowell Institute, and elsewhere, by one of the most eminent of our scholars, who is both theologian and historian. His lectures were entitled "The Divine Origin of Christianity indicated by its Historical Effects." With a profound admiration for Christianity, in whose service, under whose command, he had spent many industrious years, he declared his belief, and I think he made those who heard him in three cities believe, that the work which Christianity has done proves its divinity. His feeling had been well expressed in the words of an illustrious man, honored in many lands, "The thorough interweaving of all the roots of Christianity with the history of the world out of which it has sprung is at once a source of its power and an assurance of its divineness." About the same time another valuable book appeared, written by a man abundantly qualified for the work. It was called "Gesta Christi; or, A History of Human Progress under Christianity." With these works in your hands there is little for me to say. But I may mention by title some of the results of this movement whose beginning was so very simple and unpromising, and the vast meaning and reach of the words should be noticed. These facts were enforced and illustrated in the lectures: Christianity has given a new conception of God, finer, higher, diviner, as Father and Love; not enthroned on inaccessible heights in "a chilling and cheerless solitude," but where the cry of a child can reach Him. It has given a new conception of man, exalting his nature, raising him to his place in the world, endowing him with liberty and honor; making the lowest of account and the poorest rich. It gave a new idea of the duty of man toward God; of man's duty to man, in politics and society; of the duties of nations toward each other. It has affected the mental culture of mankind, and its effect can be seen in the world's hope of progress. If this list of chapters can sustain itself, as it was thought to do, Christianity has indeed moved on by a Divine force for the advancement of the world. Imagine any one attempting to demonstrate in ten hours that any other religion the world has ever known has been able or desirous to carry man upward and forward along these lines! "You have heard of the ten great religions of the world," remarks a brilliant preacher and a teacher of history. "Of these only three have been expansive and conquering religions. . . . And as between the three, . . . the hard, historic fact is, that Christianity is certainly carrying the day."

Let me extract a few words from the other work. The influence of Christianity has been greatly helpful in the home; it is "pure religion breathing household laws;" for the father and his authority, for woman and her child. It has made law wiser and more humane over life and property, and over the slave. It has affected public and private war. It has advanced and created education and promoted reform. It has favored science and art. There was need of all this, else it could not have been done. There was need of a great deal more. We can at least appreciate the effects which we can trace to the faith from Jerusalem.

One could hardly help being aware that it is charged upon the Church that it opposed scientific study and its results. This would not be a fatal charge, if it were true. But it is a matter with which I am not concerned, for I am not presenting the Church for your confidence, but Christianity. The scientific method does not confuse terms so distinct. They are related, but they are not the same, and have never been the same.

The Church has had its own work, and it is not surprising that in its devotion to this in the past it had little interest in scientific studies, or even feared them and opposed them. The Church was young, inexperienced, foolish. But it lived and learned. It has certainly learned. The Church of necessity felt the influence of Rome and received of its spirit, and Rome was not in sympathy with scientific inquiry. "The spirit of the naturalist did not exist among the Romans any more than it did among the Hebrew people." Whatever may have been the hesitation of the Church, no system of religion has looked with more favor upon scientific inquiry, or given it richer reward. Paganism certainly has not evoked or fostered it. What was the science of the best of the ancient nations in extent, method, accuracy, as measured by the standards of our time? I do not refer to modern discoveries, but to spirit and promise. As for opposition, is not that the fault of the times rather than the ecclesiastical authorities? Did they object to the conclusions which alarmed them because they belonged to the Church, or because they belonged to a benighted world not yet able to recognize its prophets?

Was it because they were Christians, or because they were men, that they cherished the superstitions which now amuse us? There was Roger Bacon in the thirteenth century, a Franciscan friar, but a seer, who saw the coming of science and foretold its work; the precursor, he has been called, of Francis Bacon, and Newton, and Erasmus, and Bentley. Yet he told of flying dragons in Ethiopia, which men saddled and bridled, and killed when they had ridden the flesh tender, and then ate that they might ward off the accidents of age. "They prolong life and refine the intellect beyond all belief." I do not know that he opposed any one in his discoveries. But he lets us see the confusion of the time, in which even a minister might be mistaken; a time where were wild superstitions, lawless vagaries, with fear and resistance when new theories threatened those which held the ground. That was not the spirit of the new faith, but the disposition against which it had to contend.

Lecky tells us that "the belief that the king's touch can cure scrofula flourished in the most brilliant periods of English history. It was asserted by the Privy Council, by the Bishops of two religions, by the general voice of the clergy in the palmiest days of the English Church, by the University of Oxford, and by the enthusiastic assent of the people." This was the delusion of the period, not the teaching of Christianity, which at length put an end to the superstition.

Christianity desires to appropriate all that is good, and can use it in the service of mankind. Whatever advances the material well-being of man works in its behalf. It requires good government, it fosters learning; it must employ wealth, and looks with favor upon the industry which produces it; it seeks the best literature; it encourages science; it depends upon art for its temples and their adornment, and through forms of beauty it presents the truths of the Spirit.

I cannot do better than repeat the recent words of a most accomplished Church historian: "Science only exists where Christian institutions have prepared the way for its advent; and it builds upon the conviction which the miracle has aided to develop, that nothing is impossible to man in his struggle with nature in order to clothe himself with its power and to subdue its forces to the control of the human will." If Christianity quickens the mental powers, promotes discovery, enlarges knowledge, why should it not do the same work in regard to the spiritual faculties, and quicken and elevate the life? If this is what comes of falling under Christ's control, reason compels us to yield ourselves to the influence so long as there is more good to be received. On the other hand, Christianity is to be benefited by all the advance of learning and science. What has not been done oppresses us. What has been done immediately concerns us.

I claim, in my turn, that the work of Christianity is evidence of its Divine character and mission. One thing is certain: this is the religion to which the world must look. There is no other quarter which gives the promise of light. Is not this evidence? The work before us is immense. Estimates in such matters are not of much account. But if I may express an opinion, the work which Christianity has yet to do is less difficult than that it has already done; and the way before it is less uncertain, and its resources of wisdom are larger than it has used in the past.

The beginning of Christianity when it set out upon its work was very natural. Those who were next to the Master began this ministry to the world. We have very brief accounts of their journeys and experience. The New Testament chronicles tell us nearly all we know. For the greater part they were soon lost to sight, though their light was shining in dark places. St. Peter and St. John we know, and their work. They had a preëminence which has given them the title of Saint. Saint Paul was the chief missionary, but helpers were given to him, and upon these passed the great name of Apostle. They worked with order and prudence, and with an aim at stability. Everywhere men believed. After a time they became formally organized, with all the appointments for work and worship. The manner in which this was effected is not known, but it was done. Apparently it was not done at any one time, but by degrees. Methods were hidden in the life. More care was taken to do the work than to transmit an account of it. It was natural that the early churches should be affected by the life around them, and under its influence should fashion their own methods. The institutions of the Empire might be expected to give the idea of government. The literary and philosophical spirit of Greece, in whose language the New Testament was written, gave forms of thought and expression to the new faith. "The Roman genius for government and administration, Greek philosophy, and the ancient mysteries of Oriental origin . . . constituted, as it were, the language which Christianity must adopt, if it was to make the conquest of the Empire for Christ." Great good was accomplished by means of organization. But it was not all good. A way was opened for ambition and contention, and we come very soon upon dark pages of history.

The churches grew in dimensions and importance. If the new companies gained anything by taking on dignity and claiming a share in national affairs, they certainly lost very much in parting with their simplicity. Their real force was spiritual, and this is seldom aided by arms and authority, by wealth and rank. As one wittily said, the time came when the Church was not forced to confess that it had no silver and gold; but it was able no longer to bid a lame man rise up and walk. The croziers became golden and the persons who held them wooden, it was remarked. Then came divisions, tyrannies, persecutions, and a host of confusions and oppressions. It is sad reading; and all the worse that a splendid opportunity was misunderstood. The spirit of the first days was lost or lessened. Not all consented to unchristian deeds. There were protests, efforts at resistance, separations, reformations. The life and the truth were never disowned, never lost. Through the strife we hear the voice of charity and peace. In the worst times there was a "Remnant" of the good and true. It is some credit to the Church, some witness to its vitality, that it survived the conduct of its friends. Its enemies were less dangerous. Let us accept the testimony of history to the indestructibility of the Christian Church. It has moved with unbroken life from its simple beginning, through all changes within it and without it, through national revolutions and social transformations. The globe has been shaken, but the Church has not been shaken off nor shaken down. It has stood at the centre of tumult, and in it all has been firm. The gates of hell have not prevailed against it; — that was the assurance once given in Galilee. If I may change the figure, the ship has come through the storm, with her rigging worn, her masts strained, and her rudder twisted, but with her hulk seaworthy; leaking here and there, but on the whole sound.

There are bright places all along the way of the years. There are many saintly lives and many Christian deeds; with wise administrations, famous schools, devoted missions, a gracious spirit. We mark a generous hospitality, a blessed charity, a love of books and a fondness for making them beautiful, with patience and taste which have won admiration; many stately buildings, treasures of learning, and hymns which it is still a delight to sing. The churches have preserved for us the Bible and the sacraments. The gracious, helpful influences which have been named have come down with the sadder events which could not prevent them, which even give them lustre by the contrast. It is a troubled story. It shows what can be expected of men, and makes us more sure that if we are to make a great advance we must be helped from above.

In describing the early Christian life, let me copy a few sentences from an anonymous writing of the second century, a mere fragment, which gives a picture of the life of that time. "Christians are not distinguished from the rest of mankind either in territory or in speech or in habits of life. What the soul is in the body, this Christians are in the world. The soul dwells in the body, but is not of the body; so Christians dwell in the world, and are not of the world. They share every duty as citizens, and they suffer every indignity as foreigners. Every foreign country is a fatherland to them, and every fatherland is foreign to them. . . . Christians, when punished, increase more and more from day to day, so noble is the post which God has assigned to them, and which it is not lawful for them to decline."

We must turn our thoughts forward. Certainly the new faith has proved its virtue. The missionary idea which was essential in Christianity has remained in the churches. It could not be lost unless the very spirit of Christ and his teaching disappeared. The attempt to localize or nationalize his religion would be a heresy for which there could be no excuse. To claim that we alone need it, or we alone could receive it, were not becoming. The expectation cherished by the early Christians was in keeping with their instructions, and they saw in Christianity the religion for the world. They believed that it would meet every man's wants, and protect and guide his life. This was their confidence in their Lord, and it was very early justified, as the men of many nations found in the new faith that which they required. They knew that Christ was to conquer and reign. Their zeal held its force for century after century, though with irregular control, and often with no movement forward. To say that they had misapprehension concerning times and means, and that they made serious mistakes, is only to confess their limitations. The more we think upon their shortcoming, the more must we magnify the wisdom which employed the men, and with their imperfectness wrought out better results than could be found anywhere else. Their work was not to be done speedily; not so speedily as some thought. The ways of Providence are often slow. Perhaps their errors were allowed to stay the wheels of the chariot lest they should roll too rapidly. What we are to mark now is the increasing purpose, venturing from the Paschal chamber at Jerusalem, to win the world for Christ, and to give Christ to the world as its Redeemer and King. It was a magnificent intention, even as they held it, and there was leagued with it an imperial hope which has never ceased.

But what is the condition of the world to-day with regard to its religions? At the time when these Apostles entered on their work all the Christians there were could have lived in a small town. Now it is estimated that the world has a population of not far from fifteen hundred millions, of whom about one-third, or four hundred and ninety millions, call themselves Christians. Of course, millions of these are not Christians in the real sense of the word; that is, they are not personally devoted to Christ. But the vast numbers mark the extension of the name, and in this is a stupendous truth. At that time no Gospel had been written, with the story of Christ's life and his words of instruction and promise. Now, the Gospel can be placed in the hands of three-fourths of the people of the globe. In three hundred and twenty languages some portion of the Bible is now printed for the advantage of the world, that men may have the knowledge of God and his redeeming love.

Can we estimate the Christian forces? Every Christian is a force in the service of Christ. It is the condition of discipleship. By him others are to be won, and every man who is won is a new soldier of the Cross. It means this to be a Christian, as Christ bestows the name. The order is this: the Creator; the Son of Man with new life for men; multitudes of Christians in life and under the sway of the Holy Spirit to give life to the world. There are certain organizations of Christ's men which are to be regarded. There are churches, colleges, libraries, hospitals, brotherhoods, charities, in almost endless variety. The work for the world goes on, sometimes with observation, and sometimes in secret. The hope which rules is unabated. It cannot be removed until faith vanishes away. After years in the wilderness the churches have found themselves, and have regained the meaning of their life. Figures easily slip from the mind, but I use them to give some impression of the forces now engaged in this part of the service of Christ. The statistics are recent, but no longer exact. There are eleven thousand six hundred and fifty-nine men and women who are by special appointment teaching the good news of God in countries which are not their own. There are sixty-four thousand two hundred and ninety-nine who are reported as native laborers, that is, persons who have themselves been taught, and are, in their turn, teaching their countrymen. The annual income of the voluntary associations which direct this enterprise is nearly thirteen million dollars.

Let it be remarked that this money is cheerfully given without thought of return, and to those who have never been seen by the givers; to people of strange lands, whose history and ways of life are separate from ours; as the free-will offering of faith in Christ and his teaching, in the glad obedience of his command; and that those who have given their lives to this service, becoming exiles from country and home, and the things we value most, have done it in their devotion to Him, their knowledge of his truth, their experience of his love, their longing to have his name and grace made a blessing in all the earth. It is a splendid testimony to the reality of the Christian life.

All this is but a portion. These are the missions of Protestant churches. These are modern and recent. Let it be remembered that all which Protestant Foreign Missionary organizations have done was begun in the lifetime of men who live to trace the work from its beginning. The first of these is but eighty-eight years old, and the next but sixty-one. A century is a short time for large results in an undertaking of this nature. To these results should be added the extensive missions of the Roman Catholic Church. The record of the devotion, heroism, sacrifice, of the priests who have carried the Cross into the wilderness that they might by means of it save the souls of men is unsurpassed. It is a noble army which under these names has gone forth to seek and to save.

Comparisons are out of place. But the roll of our thirty-six hundred American missionaries is a list of noblemen. They are college men, select men, who could fill the places here quite as well as those who stay at home. With them are women of high attainment, of beautiful culture, of serenest courage. They are good men and women, and good-natured; able to work, and able to work with others; with a conception of their enterprise which is a constant inspiration. No civil-service rules are so strict as those under which these Christians pass. It is not to learn their belief more than their health, and disposition, and desire. It must be clear that they understand themselves, and are fitted to carry out the purpose of those who send them and support them. It is a serious matter to send missionaries abroad, to sustain them while they learn a strange language, and to invest a large hope in them, and those who do this have a right to know whom they are taking into partnership. The entire management of this enterprise is in the hands of strong men, men of business, lawyers, clergymen; and of women wise to plan, skilful to discern, patient and brave; who bring all their wisdom to bear upon the religious, social, and financial questions which press upon them. The dignity of the work is in keeping with its importance. It is impossible to give results with an approach to fulness, and they are of inferior moment while the work is steadily going on. But I find that the Protestant societies count up four thousand six hundred and ninety-four mission stations, with fifteen thousand two hundred out-stations, over a million communicants, and nearly a million persons under instruction. What is sought is that every person in the world shall know Christ and receive his help; shall learn of Him to know the Father, to do his will, to live in his favor, to have eternal life which can readily be extended to the world that comes next. The design is broad. It is not to seize a savage and snatch him from endless death; but to find the savage, or the sage, and tell him, what no man knows till he is told, at home or abroad, that the Love of God is in the earth seeking its own, that it may give them a right spirit and persuade them into life, which is the gift of Love.

This Christian enterprise recognizes whatever good it finds, whatever of truth and faith, and making the most of this, in an economical spirit, adds to it more truth, higher truth, the Truth. These men have not consecrated themselves to a wearisome failure, and they intend to deserve the success for which they strive.

They know what they believe, and they believe that it is worth any man's knowing. They work rationally and discreetly. It is not proposed to transplant our Western system of thought and of life, and our institutions as they have been made for ourselves; but in their own language to present to men the Son of Man, and to persuade them to acknowledge Him as Master and Lord; and to make their own philosophy and set up their own organizations, and to order their affairs after their own judgment. New England Christians are in place here. But we cannot expect the Chinaman to become a New Englander. Let him retain his Oriental habit of mind and hold it in allegiance to the one Teacher. The design is to build up a kingdom on the earth, including all nations and peoples, where the will of God shall be done as it is in heaven.

It is not proposed that all this shall be accomplished by missionaries. Their work is to begin; to teach what they have learned, and to let this do its own work. They are to raise up in every country men of the land who shall minister to their own people. They are to make Christians of the New Testament order, in which every man who learned was to repeat the truth to his neighbor. Let me remark again, it is literally the method of the leaven and the seed. There is a natural limit, therefore, to the undertaking, and one which need not be far away.

We may not overlook the variety of the benefits which these men confer. They are by no means confined to things unseen and eternal. They are students and teachers. Geography, ethnology, history, sociology, philology, every department of knowledge, is indebted to them. They represent their country, and with honor. Their service to the people whom they seek, given in their daily life, is manifold and inestimable.

There has recently died in England a Christian, a Prussian by birth, who had expended seven million dollars in the care of orphan children, for more than forty thousand of whom he had provided a home, and this large amount of money had been given to him by Christian men and women, without solicitation, in their knowledge and approval of his work of faith and charity. This is an instance of one man's usefulness through a free and bold Christian confidence. The method and result are altogether in keeping with the spirit which controlled the enterprise. The whole design is distinctively Christian. It may be seen all along the centuries since Christ blessed the children. That which we call Christianity would forfeit its right to the name if it did not seek to bless men in this present world as the accompaniment of endless blessing. It was a beautiful testimony which the simple islander gave to the spirit of the missionary Patteson when his life had been taken from him by the mistaken savages for whom he lived: "He loved them all alike." I do not know of better reading than the memoirs of our missionaries, for those who would see a really Divine, Christ-like manhood in its grandeur. They give life and give it abundantly. They count nothing dear unto themselves if they can help others with it. They carry the wealth of the richest lands into those which are poorest. They create manhood. They teach law and liberty, good order and safety.

They make homes, elevate women, gladden children, save life and make it worth saving. They carry medicine and surgery, and all the useful arts. The African chief who exulted when he saw a plough, because it would save him five wives, offers a gross type of a man who felt better off. Imagine the advantage to the Dark Continent of having David Livingstone within it! We need not inquire too carefully for the consequences. Duty does not depend upon that. But in any case no one can doubt the worth to a land of having the men and women whom we call missionaries live in it, with no other design than to do the people good.

Great things have been done. But let me repeat, much more has been effected in taking up the work, getting it in hand, learning how to do it, getting established on the ground. The day of experiments is over. Investments are made, in men, in buildings, in churches and schools, in methods, in brave lives which have remembrance. It was the thoughtful statement of one of the scholarly leaders in this movement, called early from the work which needed him, and which he needed, that "Christianity has now become naturalized everywhere among the most diverse nations," and "everywhere demonstrates its character as the one religion for the human race." It has reached the highest and the lowest, and has proved its grace and truth. It is a pleasant picture which Drummond gives of an African who had become Christ's man: "He was neither bright nor clever; he was a commonplace black; but he did his duty and never told a lie. I looked out of my tent; a flood of moonlight lit up the forest, and there, kneeling upon the ground, was a little group of natives, and Moolu in the centre conducting evening prayers." His "life gave him the right to do it. I believe in missions, for one thing, because I believe in Moolu."

But religion does not work alone. It is in the world where national changes may combine to its advantage. Nothing is too great or too small for its use. Greece gave to the Good News a language, and Rome a world. The finding of this Western Continent gave a new place to the young life, a new vantage-ground from which to reach over the earth. In "rectifying boundaries" more may be accomplished than is designed. We cannot look upon the devious ways of nations with an intelligent confidence. Still, changes are certain, and change suggests opportunity. Where it has a chance, the life proves its power beyond all question and does all it is asked to do. But, unfortunately, for the most part the great advances are not at present in the most important sections of the world. In the Turkish Empire its way is blocked by Mohammedanism, which never yields an inch, where cruelty has been written in blood, as it will be to the end. The red hand on the wall of St. Sophia is the seal it stamps on everything it touches. But as civilization advances even Turkey may feel it and modernize its life. Much is already being done by these men and women; by Robert College on the Bosphorus, with the American flag waving above it; and the Girls' College at Constantinople, chartered by Massachusetts; and other kindred institutions. We are making headway even there. The best friends Turkey has had are the Christian missionaries who have been found heroes in the sad days which are not yet over. It looks as if only compulsion can effect the freedom of Christianity; but in the clashing of the powers even compulsion is possible.

There have been notable successes in India. Western influences have been felt. But India has not become Christian. Its religions have lost much of their authority, but no other has taken their place. Reforms have come, but the greatest reform is from without. We are told upon the highest authority that extraordinary changes are quietly taking place in India, in the political, social, moral, and religious life of the people. The difficulties are evident and serious. India is old. She is proud, and with reason. She has her own faith. Christianity is the religion of foreigners, and foreigners who have taken away her liberty. It interferes with venerated customs and prejudices. Its method of thought is different from hers. But in all this there is nothing which must be permanent. Christianity stands with far more promise on the borders of India, and the great countries beyond, than it had at Antioch when it looked out upon the world. Sudden changes may come, are quite certain to come if we deserve them. India is under British rule. Ships from other lands are in her ports. Railroads traverse her territory. Schools are giving out their light. Christian voices from the West are eagerly heard, and books are read. It is much to look for, yet it does not seem too much, the day when India, not along her coral strands alone, but far among her hills, shall know the life of the world. Certainly, these great nations, as they stand, are not the final outcome of the purposes of Providence. Nor can we detect a nearness to what by courtesy could be called the Kingdom of heaven. Nor are there living signs of its approach. The ages must be long which unaided will bring it in. Ages will never bring it in. It is proven that this which we name Christianity will do for India and Turkey all they need, if ever it is allowed to do it. This is the affirmation of history.

I am entirely willing to present the results of missionary effort. They have been as large as we have any right to expect, when we consider how half-hearted and half-handed we have been even in these years of opportunity. It is doubtful if any effort could have completed the work rapidly. It is often thought that the first preaching and teaching were much more remunerative. Probably we overrate those early efforts. There were great difficulties then as there are now. Triumph and defeat marked those days as they do these. "History has been called an excellent cordial for the drooping courage." It was a splendid service which was rendered by those first soldiers of the Cross. But they could not cover the world, nor completely gain that which was open to them. After a hundred years at Rome, Christianity was still "a foreign superstition," "destructive," "new and noxious," perverse, and extravagant." I take Bishop Lightfoot's estimate, that in the third century scarcely more than a hundred and fiftieth of the human race were Christians. There were rapid gains following the conversion of Constantine, but there is nothing to make us feel that our spirit and our ways are inadequate to our task. If we could part with our differences, and unite our forces in a common advance, the reward would soon come, and there is nothing which could permanently resist the army which has never been conquered.

It is well for us to remember what we are. We are proud of our descent. Among our ancestors "each freeman . . . was his own house-priest; and English worship lay commonly in the sacrifice which the house-father offered to the gods of his hearth." "Life was built with them not on the hope of a hereafter, but on the proud self-consciousness of noble souls." The Christian faith early made its way to Britain, but was driven into obscurity by the invaders; and as the sixth century was closing an Italian monk with his companions landed on the island of Thanet, and Christianity began to be the religion of the realm. In the open field, for safety, the king received the strangers. In their belief they were not strangers to Bertha, his queen, whose faith commended them. England has owed much to women. "You can speak freely to my people," said the king. Presently the king was baptized, and to-day the whole world feels his faith. He did not know that he was touching the whole world. That was one of the few great events. The faith of those rude Christians was not very intelligent or very profound. But it was a beginning. A thousand years later it crossed the wide sea and established itself permanently on these shores. Hence the Republic. Every American believes in foreign missions, so far at least as his own history is concerned. Our schools, colleges, churches, governments, we owe in this measure to Italians; they are the fruit of our religion. The grateful intelligence of America is committed. I ask to have it noted, that this colossal event in the political history of the world, the forming of this Republic, without parallel or precedent, had its beginning in the name of Christianity and under its inspiration. The influence of these two English-speaking nations increases. If they will move together, in the obedience of faith, they will make a way for the Augustine of our later time, and he will walk by the Bosphorus, and along the streams of India, and over the mountains of China and Japan, bearing always the Cross of light and liberty, and everywhere Angles shall become angels.

VI

THE CHRISTIAN FORCES

THE CHRISTIAN FORCES

The forces which are to make the world the world it ought to be are now within it. Some of them have been here from the beginning, and have worked on patiently for the improvement of society and those who compose it. We have come recently to make account of these inherent powers more than in the past. Every sign of the presence of God in the world is of help to us. The tendencies of life are to be searched out, and we are indebted to those who work in that domain with fidelity and skill, and make the results our common property. I wish that they could give us more encouragement. Perhaps they will do so, for science is young. Fortunately it is daring, and boldness is another name for promise. It must be confessed that these natural processes are very deliberate. They are altogether too slow for the individual, who properly objects to being absorbed in the race, and to find the fulfilment of his life in a congeries of strangers; to be lost in the crowd. This is not selfishness nor egotism. It is self-respect. It can be cherished without compunction, seeing that it takes nothing from the well-being of remote descendants. Under the rule of Providence every one has the right to look for his own advance, and every one thinks he has fitness enough to warrant his survival. One thing is evident, that these natural forces are not accomplishing the work which needs to be done. We are by no means sure of their continuance and the happy completing of their effort. Even now they do not bring men to the knowledge of God, their Father, whose life and law are Love, and to the estate of Glory, Honor, Immortality. They do not give that new principle of life which contents a man before his own conscience and the intelligent thought of his Creator. In a word, they do not give life and renew the first creation. One speaks with caution when he alludes to the possibilities of the ages. We are soon carried to the realm of conjecture and expectation. Under other conditions we might have been glad even of hope. But we have no need to resort to it. We can keep it as a solace for imaginative hours. It is plainly not substantial enough for daily use. Happily we have a way of life which is entirely definite, and is open before the feet of every man; so narrow that no one need miss it, so wide that good men can walk abreast. The presence of God is in the world; in it, but not held to it or limited by it; in it to use his Love, wherein is the whole range of fatherly thought and desire, for the regaining and perfecting of his children. This presence of God was in its fulness manifested in his Son, the Son of Man, who has given his life for the world. The Spirit of God, that is, God who is Spirit, is in the world to persuade men into the Divine grace of the Son of Man. This is distinct. Resting here, one can welcome all additions to knowledge, every disclosure of the thought of the Creator, every bestowment of his spirit in the lives of men. His ministry of life our Lord committed to his friends, that through them all might learn of Him. On the largest scale all things would be made to work together for their good. It is not difficult to see that the teaching of the Son of Man has advanced with the course of events. We boast of the age we are living in, and not without reason; and I presume we should agree that Christ and his teaching have never been so well understood and appreciated, and never had so great influence as in this remarkable century. "There is no romance so marvellous as the most prosaic version of his history," whether this be read in the Bible or in the later chronicles of men and nations. I use the word influence in a large way; for this is felt in many places where its authorship is not confessed. Indeed, it is impossible to separate the influence of Christianity from any virtue, or any good work, which we find here. We have inherited something of its method and spirit, perhaps through generations. If we give it no personal heed, we are not free from its control. It is in the home and the school. It is in our blood, our nerves, our habit of thought and work. It is in customs, in literature, in institutions. We cannot take it out of the air we breathe. There are disciples who are unaware of their discipleship. It is like the breaking of the day when one of them finds Him in whom he has believed, and finding Him believes the more.

I am to mention one event which finds its beginning in this control, and in accomplishing the Divine purpose has the intent and honor of its being. The past and the future meet within it, and on equal terms. I have already named the formation of this Republic as an event ordered of God for the bringing in of his Kingdom upon the earth. I have no declamation upon our national greatness and honor, but history cannot be trifled with. If the presence and direction of God in the affairs of men are to be recognized, if they are a reality, it should be an easy thing to see them. In our idea of God, He is a very present help, working out the counsel of his own will. If the presence and work of the Son of Man are as real and Divine as I have claimed, then nothing which can be done among men, among nations, is too great to be made tributary to them. How can we sever such things from the thought of the Creator? The child's question was a natural one, "What does God do all day?" For myself I reply at once: God is carrying forward the ministry which entered the world when Christ was born in Bethlehem.

It was by Divine guidance — this seems to me the only rational explanation — it was by Divine guidance that Spain was warded off from this Northern coast. The continent was indeed "picked out of the ocean on the point of a needle;" but it was not brought from the obscurity of centuries for her possession. The treasure of the new continent was a sorry prize for Castile and Aragon. But it was made to serve the interest of freedom beyond all desire of its possessors. I believe the Netherland school of liberty was really founded by American gold.

A Republic is the highest form of political institution, so D'Tocqueville wrote, and we assent to it. The highest form of Republic is one made of different nationalities, brought under one government and one flag. Such a Republic was unknown, and the time came for it. Where should it be? Asia offered no field, Europe was crowded and committed, and Africa was hardly the place for an experiment so grand and difficult. This was the only land where a nation of this kind was possible. This continent had been concealed until the right men, rightly trained, could build their houses in the wilderness and hold the ground for a purpose larger than they knew. Let me give out one verse of the Boston Hymn:

> The word of the Lord by night
> To the watching Pilgrims came,
> As they sat by the sea-side,
> And filled their hearts with flame.

It was at that time, and with a clear understanding of all which was involved, that John Winthrop wrote for the "encouraging such whose hearts Gods shall move to joyne" in "the intended Plantation in New England." "It will be a service to the Church of great consequence to carry the Gospel into those parts of the world, to help on the coming of the fulness of the Gentiles." If these words of the early statesman and missionary, with the verses of the New England poet, truly record the suggestion and the intention which brought Englishmen to these shores, the historical spirit leads us to look for the continuance of the inspired and exalted purpose. I have no thought of tracing our national life. It has not been altogether according to our mind. But it has never lost the way or the course. In nearly three hundred years we have not made a serious mistake, an error of imperial proportions. Our line has wavered and been irregular, but we have gone forward. The Colonies have become a Republic, the first empire of its kind. "E pluribus unum" means of many nations one State. The Republic has cast off slavery and now stands in its strength. Perhaps this has a sound of bragging, but never mind. We have a chronic habit of living up to our boasting; and something must be pardoned to the exuberance of youth. In all parts of the land many are working together for the preserving, the strengthening, the completing, of the Republic which demands more the more it receives. But no men are doing better work than those who are in direct Christian service, and notably those who in the West and South are teaching the religion which includes virtue, industry, patriotism; and, following our own experience, are building into the nation the intelligence and piety which will be security and strength. Let us be mindful of the good which we have, and cleave to it.

Here in name, to a large degree in truth, the Creator is confessed. His law is authority, and his Providence is trusted. The name of the Son of Man and his teaching are honored. The day of his birth and of his rising from the dead are regarded. On the first day of every week his resurrection is commemorated. There is much of formality and informality in this, but it is significant that opinion and feeling are thus expressed. The events have a permanent record, though their meaning may not be considered, and the form may recover the spirit.

The influence of this country is increasing. The influence of England is everywhere felt. The two nations have one history and one language; one mission and opportunity. They reach the whole earth, and are able to extend the teaching of Christ and to present his life for the life of men. At present the hope of the world is, in good measure, in these nations, while others bear his name and pray for his Kingdom, that it may come upon the earth. We do well to remember that the latest proposal of peace was from the land of Peter the Great, who built a city on the sea to bring his people closer to the world. Still, for the present, the main dependence for leadership must be upon the English lands. Liberty, knowledge, righteousness, must go from their doors. Religion can be found everywhere; it is life the world needs. Life and light dwell together; where the free school and the free church stand in increasing strength; the right to think and the intention, the liberty, to speak, and the determination to make use of it. When we reckon numbers and count our gains we may be despondent. But when we observe where Christianity is, and with what energy it is allied, we have new hope. But the great thing is to feel that the Creator is at work, that the intention which gave Christ to the earth abides in all its strength. It is in the world, and while this is true

To doubt would be disloyalty.

In place of any prediction of my own, or my countrymen's, let me read these generous words of an English scholar: "In the centuries that lie before us, the primacy of the world will lie with the English People. English institutions, English speech, English thought, will become the main features of the political, the social, and the intellectual life of mankind. . . . In the days that are at hand the main current of that people's history must run along the channel not of the Thames or the Mersey, but of the Hudson and the Mississippi." I supplement the promise of the English historian with the words of the American statesman. The late Secretary of State said at Cambridge: "Our mission is to act. We must advance the cause of Christian charity by deeds as well as words. There is a patriotism of race as well as of country. The Anglo-American race should not forget this. They should stand together if necessary against all the world, for in their closer union lies the best type of all Christianity." Thus we send out our voice "To a people proud and free."

> And it says to them: Kinsmen, hail!
> We severed have been too long;
> Now let us have done with a worn-out tale,
> The tale of an ancient wrong;
> And our friendship last long as love doth last,
> And be stronger than death is strong.

What we term missionary work is not limited to personal effort. The enterprise is organized and known in the banks and by the government of every State. But besides this, nations are missionaries. The ships from Christian countries carry at least the name of Christ, and their movements pay heed to his life. Our navy floats the Sabbath flag in the harbors of the world. I wish I could say all this with more confidence.

I have spoken of the hope of the world and its

place in a young nation. We have little in the past, but no one can measure the years to come. To be alive and increasing, to be young and awake, this is to order the future. It cannot be constructed out of the days which are gone, or by those whose chief faculty is memory and chief pastime the admiration of ancestry. The heroes and divinities of distant periods have their place, but the present must have its own leaders. Christianity belongs in this day as truly and literally as in any period of its history. No mark of age, no sign of change, has passed upon it. The most important thing it has done in the latter half of this century is the summoning to its service the young life which has responded eagerly. On the Day of Pentecost, when the new faith started forward into all neighboring lands, it was announced that the words of the Hebrew prophet were fulfilled. They began to be fulfilled; but so far as we have any account a very important part of them was not at all regarded. The time had not come. There is perspective in prophecy. The Prophet had said, " Your young men shall see visions." " Your sons and your daughters shall prophesy." That was twenty-seven hundred years ago, but not till our own time has this been true. Now it is superbly true. A new page is written into the annals of the faith. Young men are seeing visions and declaring them. To enlist youth in the service of the faith is to make its advance certain. Young men and women in the light of the vision are united for this purpose under various names, all of which are Christian. I make no distinction between these organizations. But since I cannot describe all, let me state a few facts regarding one, and the oldest. These can be readily extended to the others. I speak now of the Young Men's Christian Association, with which should be associated that of the young women. The first association of young men was formed in London in 1844. The first in Boston was formed in 1851. Since then they have swept over the globe. In 1897 buildings were purchased for their use in Rome, Madras, Calcutta, Tientsin, Rio de Janeiro. The last report which I have gives fourteen hundred and twenty-nine associations in America, with a membership of two hundred and forty-eight thousand, seven hundred and thirty-four; with buildings and other real estate valued at seventeen million, seven hundred and seven thousand, nine hundred and fifty dollars, and with an annual expense list of more than two million and a half dollars. The figures give some idea of the dimensions to which this work has attained. All this force is for manhood, good citizenship, industry, generosity, godliness. Here are a few figures from one of our younger American cities. There are five buildings, valued at one million, eight hundred and thirty-two thousand dollars; and five thousand, nine hundred and thirty-two members. The receipts for 1897 were eighty-seven thousand, eight hundred and ninety-six dollars, and forty-two cents, a gain of more than eighteen thousand dollars over the preceding year.

This is only one department of the enterprise, which has also taken its place in colleges. The seventy thousand young men in our colleges and universities are a power which is equal to anything rational which they attempt. These associations are permanently established in about five hundred and fifty North American institutions for higher learning, which is nearly the whole. It is reported that more than one-half the students are enlisted under the name of Christ, that He may win the world. These associations are leagued together for the enhancement of their strength. President Roswell Hitchcock was so impressed with what he saw that he said, "The omnipresence, and I had almost said the omnipotence, of the Intercollegiate Young Men's Christian Association is the great fact in the religious life of our colleges to-day." A union similar to this holds nearly every great institution in England and Scotland. The wisdom and the spirit are enlarged within each body of young men, while combined effort employs and increases the separate force. With the spirit rich in courage, deep in devotion, young men have looked abroad, desiring to make the most of their life and to help the world. With only one opportunity, they have resolved to make the most of it. Another world may offer exalted employment; but this chance comes but once. They are under the vows of knighthood to be all they can, and to do all they can, "In His Name." Thousands in the United States and Canada have banded themselves together for what was once foreign work. It looked like the enthusiasm of youth. I presume that almost every person has so regarded it. It was the old-fashioned way of judging young men. This is all recent, but under this Student Volunteer movement, more than eleven hundred have already gone, as the time came when their training was complete, and the number ready to go is in excess of the means to send them. Over four thousand are now enrolled as volunteers. In view of this enrolment President McCosh exclaimed, "Has any such offering of living young men and women been presented in our age, in our country, in any age or in any country, since the Day of Pentecost?" Last year the colleges and seminaries gave forty thousand dollars for the promotion of the work. The intention is — and it is not unreasonable — that in the lifetime of this generation the whole world shall know the name of its Lord and Redeemer. They expect it. Meantime missionary literature is receiving systematic study, that men may know the work to which they are setting their hands. General Armstrong said, with his usual sagacity, that it is easier to get men than money. But for this enterprise the money will come. We are preparing a generation of givers. I mark that the Day of Pentecost, which promised the young men, culminated in money enough for all the wants of the new community.

There is more to tell. The Christian Associations have established themselves in all lands, and are in fellowship, nation with nation. They are in the colleges of the world, and these are now united. In August, 1895, at the old Castle of Vadstena, on Lake Wettern, in Sweden, there was a conference attended by men from America, Britain, Germany, Scandinavia, and from mission countries strictly so called, to consider the union of the unions of the world. The result was the World's Student Christian Federation. Seven hundred student associations are included in this union, which reaches India and Ceylon, China and Japan, Australasia and South Africa. Its design is to unite the Christian students of all nations, and so far as it is possible to win all other students, and by this means to give Christ and his teaching to the world, in the confidence that if He is lifted up He will draw all men to Himself. Universities have often been the source of religious life, the centres of religious movements, and it will be so again. Students are accessible to students. There is a fellowship between college men which is natural and practical. They are a guild. A student in India or China is the friend of the student from England or America. The thought and life of the newer world will reach the older lands through the doors of the college, and by the hearts of young men which have felt the hearts of their fellows. A recent foreign tour in the interest of this movement led to twenty-two countries and a hundred and forty-four schools and colleges. More than fifty-five hundred delegates were met, of whom thirty-three hundred represented three hundred and eight higher institutions of learning. At a Christian conference in India there were fifteen hundred delegates, and they were keen, bright men. Let it be understood that this banding and enlisting of students has for its immediate end the extension of Christianity over the world. It is Home Mission work. Christian students are to evangelize their own countries. It is the work of men who have an inherited respect for all that is good in their national faith, who are in sympathy with their people and devoted to their country.

The work is entirely in unison with that which has prepared the way for it. The veterans will see their labor rewarded. Sowers and reapers will rejoice together. The undertaking is vast and difficult, but the power which moves in it is patient and resistless. There is here an advance which dignifies the century. Its look is forward. It has time in its hand and courage in its heart. It holds the future.

It may be asked if Christian work is needed abroad where nations have their own religion. It is reported that there are fifty million slaves in Africa to-day, held by savages. Five hundred thousand die each year under this cruel life. They are taken in battle, and in trade. Slaves are current money. Parents barter their children, and children provide for their parents by selling them. The owners are religious. They give their slaves in sacrifice to their gods. When they are hungry they eat them. Oh, yes, they have a religion of their own! What right have foreigners to meddle with it? Some young Americans, without much regard for the religious privileges and pleasures of the slave land, have gone out there to make their homes, thinking to change the social customs of the people. Conscious of a divine life within them, they propose to impart it. A small piece of leaven goes a long way when once it gets into the meal. A thousand miles off its influence is less evident. If suffering is the same thing in Africa as in Cuba, just now we favor this intervention, and all the more that it goes with the Cross, and not the sword.

How noble is all this uprising of young life! Every profession here is full, and will easily be kept full by those who have no call to go abroad. But it is a fine ambition which ranges beyond a pent up Utica. These young men and women are free. No traditions detain them. They are committed to nothing but the Truth. They have one Lord, and Him alone they call Master. They bear many names, but one is supreme. They have the ardor of youth, with the discipline of study. They are the soldiers of a young leader. The world is theirs if they want it, and they do want it. They follow the cross in the sky, and will conquer.

> My Knights are sworn to vows
> Of utter hardihood, utter gentleness,
> And, loving, utter faithfulness in love,
> And uttermost obedience to the King.

President Eliot explains the concern which universities feel for the permanence of religious institutions: "Universities exist to advance science, to keep alive philosophy and poetry, and to draw out and cultivate the highest powers of the human mind. Now, science is always face to face with God, philosophy brings all its issues into the one word — duty; poetry has its culmination in a hymn of praise, and a prayer is the transcendent effort of intelligence." It is admirably said. The well-chosen words ask of us an unlimited extension. It is in the Christian life they will have their liberty. If it is well to be face to face with God, then is the science which Christ taught, wherein men see God, of inestimable worth. If duty is a supreme word, duty as Christ taught it, with his precepts and in his life, comes with profoundest meaning and authority. If praise is comely and to be everywhere rendered, the gift of Christ, of his love, of Himself, is the inspiration of the loftiest and sweetest songs. If prayer is the "transcendent effort of intelligence," then it is to learn of Christ, and to take to itself the deepest emotions of the soul, in penitence, thankfulness, faith, and the desire for God.

Christianity would breathe through the university, through the soul of every teacher and every scholar, "the power of an endless life." Knowledge would be higher, ambition nobler, life more Divine. The glory of scholarship is in its use; the highest glory is the highest use. Nothing will "draw out and cultivate the highest powers of the human mind" so well as the Spirit and the teaching of the Truth and the Life, who brings to the mind the largest incitement and uplifting, and makes known the highest knowledge, not otherwise attainable, and gives to all knowledge the delight of holy service. Christ takes away nothing good, and withholds nothing which is to be desired.

All this which has been said enters into the thought and plan of the young Christians who have devoted their life to the service of Christ in the world for which He gave Himself. One part of their work has been presented. There are many other parts under different names, but with the same design. The men are well known and highly esteemed. By business methods, by enterprise, by sincerity, by hard work, by faith and love, they have made themselves a power in the world; a power which increases from year to year.

Think how very largely the young men and women, the boys and girls, of the land are united for Christian service. They are trained in this. I do not know that everything they have done has shown the wisdom of age. That would not be desirable. It is the privilege of youth to have a hopeful daring in feeling and action. They study and are taught, but the grand aim is the Christ life, and He pleased not Himself. To-morrow they will be men and women. They are the future. They cannot be counted; they cannot be diverted. One could almost smile at fears, and warnings, and sad prophecies, and the proffer of strange beliefs, imported dreams, exhausted mysteries. The men of to-morrow hear nothing, care nothing, for all this. Why, the future is here! Christianity moves quietly, steadily forward. It has already taken possession of the next fifty years. The boy can be trusted. We remember how finely he came to the rescue when the hungry multitude gathered around Christ and there was no bread to give them. When He worked one of his signs He had something to begin with. That day He had nothing. A boy was there, with a few barley cakes and small fishes, which his foresight had brought for his ever-recurring condition. He gave them up, — I do not know why except that he was a boy, — and in the Lord's hands they became a feast, and more. It is true still; the boy holds the loaves. By his wealth and his consent the world is to be fed. Already he has placed his gift in the Teacher's hands. The bread is provided. The people will not be sent into their villages. The proportions are not discouraging — one boy, five barley loaves, two fishes, and five thousand men, beside women and children. I think the terms are not against us, even with the twelve men added. We, too, have Christ.

If the claim for Christianity which has been asserted is well founded, if it is the Divine method for the recalling of men, then it must prevail. We need energy, enterprise; to invest ourselves in our plans; to vitalize our forms; to prove that the new is more efficient than the old. When this comes the world will feel it. Of one thing we can see the evidence at any hour: the power of the faith by which the man is brought into contact with Christ, so that the Divine life is breathed into his life. This is the work of the Holy Spirit, and by his grace the taking possession of the life of God. That this may be done, Christ should be known; that the soul may be opened before Him, and that He may impart his own nature. "With a vital warmth which is ascending" the new life is taken, and lived into clearer light. The one essential thing is, that the life of the Son of Man be given to men by the Spirit of life.

What is claimed for this faith is found in it. It will take a man who is selfish, without regard for God or man, and will make him thoughtful, generous, upright, with a prayer in his heart and a song upon his lips. It is not his own work, though it is with his desire. It comes with his submission to the will of Christ. But it is the work of the Divine Spirit in his spirit. There is another man, with a new life, and one which lasts. I give this at the best; but it is the best which it is prepared to do. All this has been done. It is the commonplace among men who teach the way of life in the cure of souls. There are variations, but the method itself, and the result itself, are the same the world over. It would be safe to assure any man who will thus commit himself to Christ and his Spirit that he will become what has been termed "a new man." If this can be effected, as it has been, what remains but that every man be taught these things, and brought where they will become true in his own experience? The work of recovery which is necessary is already accomplished in myriads of souls. What shall we strive for but its completion? The work needs to be done. Nothing else is doing it. This is doing it. The future is provided for. What do we need more? Force.

It is not designed to put man back where he was. These years have been too costly, and we must have the good of them. A man is taken in his strength, with all he has acquired, with all he has learned, and while he bows before the incarnate Love he is invested with new energy, a new purpose, a true heart, a new commandment, a clear light; and thus purified, invigorated, directed, he is set in the right path and led down the ages. In this world, in any world, he lives in the newness of life. If this is the Divine way, this should be the result. If this is the result, it should be the Divine way. It is the result.

It is a matter of quantity now. The problem is no longer difficult, and it is not beyond our reach. The loom which will weave a piece of cloth can cover the globe. It is a question of power, not of looms. What has been done in Jerusalem can be accomplished in Galilee. Nazareth can witness the works of Capernaum. We have finished experiments. These are the days of repetition.

If I were preaching, I should urge some points more strongly. Even now, let me add a few considerations which may enforce what has been written. In this day when the scholarly and scientific spirit prevails, if a free and generous temper is to rule, Christianity deserves the honest thought of every man. It has its philosophy, which is entitled to respect. It is not a matter of emotion, though it engages the deepest feeling. It is not an experience alone, though it enters into all life. It has its history which is well defined, and its rational principles which are readily discerned. It reaches into the unseen and infinite. It must do this, or stop. But it is concerned with the present, its duties, relations, necessities, opportunities. It offers itself to this world and here makes proof of its strength. Any appeal can make promises and safely postpone the day of payment. If it puts this far enough off, it can maintain its credit. Any system of religion which expects to be believed should begin all its work at once and where it can be tested. For it is in this, as really as in any sphere, that religion is needed. Christianity begins here, and at a moment's notice. It does not complete its work, for that stretches on forever. It gives to-day what to-day requires, and never ceases to give. We do not know all it means perfectly. That were too much for the first hundred years, but the Divine care which seeks us and receives us never gives us up. It does not supplant our energy, but employs it. It permits and encourages our personal intercourse with the Creator.

There is more in religion than being blessed: there is God. Our spiritual nature is enlarged and elevated as we walk with Him. The mercantile considerations which at times enter into our views of religion are not creditable. If we are true men we desire to be with God, with our mind and heart fixed on Him. When we are there we breathe out our desires and construct our life in the simplicity of children.

The philosophy of the Christian life requires that we live in the thought of the Son of Man; in his thought of us, which is certain, and in our thought of Him; and that will keep the steady inflowing of the Divine life. This cannot be taken once for all. The prayer is exact when it says "our daily bread." The true bread from heaven must be "daily bread." It is never to leave our mind that the Christian is one who belongs to Christ; who draws his life from Him; who believes Him and believes in Him; who finds freedom in obedience. " Where the Spirit of the Lord is there is liberty."

Many excellent traits belong to the Christian, but are not confined to him, and do not describe him. He is more, in that he is the disciple and apostle of Him from whom the name comes. To use the name Christian without reference to Him is to break the laws of language. There is no narrowness in defining the term, for any one can bear it who wishes. Christianity embraces all the virtues and holds them in one design. Life is not made in sections. Its method is simple, beautiful, Divine. Our Father is spirit, and we are therefore spirit. This is our lineage. Then comes the honest life, true to itself and its source in the Spirit, constantly coming to us, constantly received and lived. To teach the Divine goodness and mercy to every man in the world is the privilege of those who have learned the truth. Thus the kingdom of heaven is coming on the earth. For themselves and for the world men are to live in Christ, because the Divine life in the fulness of its grace and truth is his. Let it be remembered that it is Himself Christ gives, not his influence. It is himself the man gives, not his confidence. Two lives meet and the one prevails over the other and persuades it into a new nature. The union is for life, and life is endless. An English writer calls it " the essential weakness of all mere systems of morality, and of most, if not all, other religions, that they confine themselves to pointing out what the facts of life ought to be, and make no provision whatever for dealing with facts as they are." The Son of Man came into the world knowing it perfectly and longing to serve it. He came down from his home among the hills and dealt with the facts which surrounded Him. He went into the misery and sin of the earth, into its hypocrisy and oppression. He offered freedom. He gave the Truth. He taught righteousness. He told men that He had come to save them and that He must die in doing it. This was his passion, and He never faltered. There is no explanation of this life but his own, and He explains the thought of the Father. One is startled at Doctor Holmes' cry, "How can God bear it! This ball of anguish forever spinning before Him, and the great hum of its misery going up to his ears." He does not bear it. In his Son He comes into it, and offers to every man his hand to bring him out of it, and every man shall speedily escape from it who wills to have it so. The pain at the world's misery is lightened by the joy of taking it away. Already where his mercy has been carried we account it a very pleasant thing to live, and heaven itself rarely attracts one away. The world is not a "ball of anguish;" and it can have less misery any day it decrees it. We are standing in the love of God when we believe in a highway out of sorrow and sin. "I am the way," He said.

I have presented to you the purpose and promise of Christ. I wish to give a resistless influence to all I have written by letting other men say it. This truth must have its proof in the life, and it may be seen in life which we honor even now that it is removed from our sight. I name two or three men of exalted character, whose sincerity and wisdom are unquestioned, whose philosophy is in the foremost thinking of scholars; who were sagacious, careful, scientific, critical, and who could not well be mistaken in questions of personal experience, and to whom pretence was impossible. The religious principles of such men deserve respect because they are such men. There are many of whom my words are true who have tested Christ and his teaching under varied conditions, and whose faith in Him dignified their noblest years. I think of the president of a great college, Theodore Woolsey, a man whose presence was a benison as he crossed the yard. He was well trained in life, a lawyer, theologian, professor. He was an eminent Greek scholar, and one of the revisers of the New Testament. He lived in the present, familiar with all times. He wrote on international law, political science, civil liberty, socialism. He kept his life young among young men, and he built no wall around his thought. He believed in his soul. He kept it open before spiritual light and grace. He let it range the ages. He was an old man when he reached his "time of graduation," as he gently called it. Then, honored by a countless number of scholars, he ascended to other, perhaps not higher, service. Was the opinion of this man on subjects with which he was well acquainted of decided value? Now, this man believed, on literary and personal grounds, that the four biographies of Christ are trustworthy. He was probably uncertain over some point in a Greek manuscript; but he believed the record. He went much farther. He believed this so thoroughly that he accepted the teaching of Christ, and held it to be the Truth. He looked to Him for guidance, for knowledge, for righteousness of life. He trusted the promises he read, and believed that Christ would win the world. He did more than this, much more. If he had been asked — he said it without being asked — what highest desire he had for the thousands of young men who revered him, and whose lives were for four years and longer in his keeping, he would have replied with all the solemnity which many and industrious days could impart: I would that every young man who enters the gates of this college should be the thorough-going disciple of Jesus Christ, receiving his words as they are written in the New Testament, and seeking his Spirit as the only inspiration.

Change the form, but not much, and this is true of our Harvard saint, whose thought of Christ has been already told. To him were given a lofty character, wide learning, broad influence, a large part among men. He was called to be the teacher of young men; and from his words, even more from the man himself, they took lessons in life, and they desired to live. To talk with him was to respect him and to respect yourself. He carried many in his sympathies, and all the long way he was telling men to be the scholars and the true friends of Christ; to trust Him perfectly, and to make up life entirely by his rules.

With him stands my own President at Harvard, James Walker; the wise man, the great man; the writer and teacher of philosophy; the vigorous preacher; who made the reading of the Bible at morning prayers something to be talked about when we had left the chapel; who adorned the truth he taught. I can hear to-day the impressive roll of his strong voice, intense in its honesty: "Young men, you have much more need of religion than religion has of you." Those who recognize the man will mark how well he described himself in these words: "There is no ignoring, there is no concealing, the inconveniences, the infirmities, which steal over us as we descend into the vale of years. . . . It is a great thing to be surrounded by kind friends and all the endearments and appliances of a happy home. But greater than all, 'to know Christ, and the power of his resurrection,' as a hope full of immortality." With this hope an old man still has "something to live for, and something to die for."

The men come rapidly when we start to think upon them. It was not long ago — it was very long ago — that one walked among us whom all men honored. It was a stately presence. It needed to be for the soul it sheltered. What man has drawn to himself the homage of the place as did he who never sought applause? He knew no boundaries of heart or help. He was the minister of Trinity; but no church could confine him. He held the souls of men in thrall. Every one knew the way to his open door. His years were not many, but they were large. His words were in all lands, his voice at the ends of the earth. Yet chiefly here where we saw him every day was he honored and loved. It was a rare fame, unsullied as he rose to high station. How great he was! How good! What made it all? Was it learning, eloquence, kindness, humanity, a large manhood in rare opportunities? These indeed were his. But these were not the man. No one knows him who has not gone beneath all this, and found him. He was a Christian. He profoundly believed in Christ. He lived with Him, in Him. He walked in his light and worked in his strength. He was large-hearted, but there was not a desire in the whole range of his feeling which was so strong, persistent, universal, as the longing that every man whom he could by any means persuade should live in the grace of Christ's words, and be guided, purified, ennobled, by his indwelling Spirit. If he could consent to any honor, and could choose what it should be, he would place above all other distinction the glory of standing before the world a witness to the truth of the religion which he taught and lived.

I do not claim that Christianity is true because these men believed it, and in their lives put it to the proof. But I do claim that it is entitled to reverent and hopeful study, and to personal allegiance, when it has commended itself to the conscience and the life, as these teachers say that it will. I could enlarge the catalogue of names almost without bounds, and from all the ways of life. But what need of this?

These witnesses, multiplied by thousands of intelligent and honest men, encourage the confidence which comes with the very presence of Christ and in every word He taught, that this religion will meet men in their want, teach them what they need to learn, empower them for that which they have to do. No want has yet been discovered to which Christianity does not effectively address itself. It is distinctly ethical, and the principles of morality are the same the world over. The Ten Commandments, the two commandments, are valid on every spot the sun shines upon. There is no place where they do not make for virtue, happiness, peace, helpfulness, and length of days. It does more than teach duty. It provides the motive and desire to do it, and it furnishes the moral strength. It is life. Beyond the doing, this religion is religious. It knows God. We cannot fail to notice the virility of this religion. This is found in its spirit and its requirements; it is seen in the practical evidence of its power which is everywhere. It makes men. There is not a dreamy, speculative line in all its precepts. It is gentle and kindly, but rugged and solid. Its moral and spiritual energy is manifest. Everywhere it gives vigor to the will, force to the affections, temper to the soul, and makes the conscience robust. It excepts nothing from its authority, not even eating and drinking. It excludes nothing from recognition, not even a cup of water or a drop of oil. In its idea all of life is sacred. It writes on the bells of the horses the inscription on the high priest's helmet. It finds room in its service and its records for St. Paul and Dorcas both. All this is religion, but it is not the whole of religion, which must stand in the thought of God, in unity with Him, in love, in trust, in the desire and intent to do the things which please Him, and because they please Him. When conduct parts with God, it is no longer religious. Thus religion makes life more interesting and honorable at the same time that it unites it with the Divine life; and it makes the thoughts and feelings more exalted when it enshrines them in the common duties which it requires and rewards, and which the world needs. To make all this real and assured the Son of Man lives in men. They know his presence and they offer it the love which fosters piety and yields obedience in good works. In his own words of friendliness, they sup with Him and He with them. Faith, Hope, Love abide. They have immortality and more. Eternal life is more. It is offered to every man, forced on no one. Christ did not come to destroy, but to save, and He does not destroy life in the act of saving it; removing its liberty to secure its happiness. His gifts are from freedom to freedom. Life is to live. The breath of the Almighty was not given to be withdrawn. Our days are not to end in a vanishing point. We do not hold them at the will of change and chance. The Son of Man gave Himself, not to perfect seventy years, but to perfect life. He restored man because man was to live. We take the grandeur away if we think this is not so. For the Creator to withdraw man to Himself is to lose. From everlasting He had the life and He added man. By this personality He gained. To bring this to an end would be to cancel his own thought and destroy his own work. He would lose a child.

If He takes the man's life back into his life, there is no more life than before, and the man is gone. There is less to love. "Not vitality, but personality, is the witness for immortality," Asa Gray wrote. Christ came to make pure the enduring heart of man, and to make his life like God's. There was inducement to this in the endless years. All the way the scale is Divine. We think we were "not made to die," and God has made us. He will make life a blessing in the Son. There is a tradition that St. Paul wished he had met Virgil. We may share his regret. I wish that Christ could have met Buddha. He would have enlightened him, fostered all that was noble and kind in him, lifted his burden of sorrow and his pain for the world, carried him in heart and hope past Nirvana into Paradise. Life would have been a blessing to be cherished, and immortality an unspeakable joy. I wish He could have seen the man so greatly loved, and have taken him for a disciple and apostle!

We have a natural interest in the world, and in whatever will help it to know itself and enjoy its life. It is not a deserted world. If we call it lost, as there is warrant for doing, we must also call it found. If we think it prodigal, and well we may, it has not wandered out of the care of Him who made it. The work of the Divine life in the world has gone far, but it is far from completion. Many difficulties are surmounted, but others remain, and they are real, whatever be their form, however slight they seem. If the coral insects built the Dolomites, it is only good climbing which surmounts them. We say that the world is open before the messengers of God. Not quite. They can go into any land, but not into every heart. The call "From Greenland's icy mountains" is not more strong than when Hans Egede answered it two hundred years ago. Nevertheless the Divine faith is advancing, and the Divine presence moves before it, cloud by day and fire by night. We plan for the world, but we cannot forget the need along our own streets, in our hovels and palaces, on the hills and by the streams. If the result were better here we should have more readiness to extend the good. There is a serious thought in the questions of an American historian: "Christianity has conquered all the best races in history thus far. Now, can it conquer to the bottom, as it has already conquered to the top? Can it bring the whole human family, its lowest peoples with its highest, into one common fold? Can it evangelize its own cities, going down into the cellars, up into the garrets, of its own heathens here at home? Hard as the task may be, Christianity stands squarely committed to it. What it can do may be known from what it has done."

If things have been done by those bearing this name, which have had little of the spirit of the Teacher, we knew they were not of his bidding. We said the treasure is in earthen vessels, but we knew that the treasure was true. If we had confused vessel and treasure we had been careless, or worse. But always the faith itself can be found. The treasure is not to be hidden in vessels. The broken alabaster is to let the spikenard send out its fragrance. The box needs no cover, and the world needs the perfume. One may see at Naples a joint of pipe from Pompeii with the water still within it. You shake this and the water answers, but it cannot escape. It is a curiosity, but not a benefit. Let the faith escape from men and schools and it will live. To live is the normal state of life, to live and to give life.

The life of the Son of Man has not entrenched itself in castles and palaces, claiming regal honors, asserting political authority, and subduing kings. It has lived in meekness and gentleness; teaching good-will, breathing out charity, healing, comforting, restoring; revealing God and calling men home. Whatever else appears, this reveals itself. It lives in this grace now. If we could agree to take this as the rule of life, the world would feel its power. The world, which gets too little help from stately institutions, would find its streets lighted by his presence and its waters levelled under his feet. I beg that Christ and his truth may not be judged by the things which men have done against which our humanity cries out. Let not those be overlooked in whom the spirit of Christ has done a more perfect work. There are men on whom the name of saint is not unbecoming; men and women in whom a high-minded charity has lived, who have made the world beautiful, and have lived in the presence of the Lord, in the power of his Spirit. May not Christianity be judged by its best? It has its best, of whom the world was not worthy, and they were its light — often solitary, as beacon lights are wont to be.

The best is the real. There have been brave deeds, easily recalled; great thoughts and forces. There was wonderful strength in the old forms of Christian belief which have lessened their power. They made God great and his sovereignty strong, and we need that work to-day. Calvinism "set its face against illusion and mendacity," as Froude says; and it produced vigorous characters, equal to large achievements. That system will not return, but the virtue which was in it cannot perish.

Who shall call men and churches to the way of

life, and bring us in contentment around the one name? Perhaps no one. Yet in some form the truth of Christ is to find men and to save them. I sometimes fancy that such a man is coming. Not yet. The time is not ready for him. If he comes, it will be in Spirit and in power; he will find the good and value it; he will give honor to the churches and their service; he will be tolerant and generous; he will not strive nor cry, but quietly, with Divine power, he will persuade, and the conscience of men will approve, and they will receive the Divine life for themselves, for the country, for the world. He shall live. In his heart "shall dwell visions of a world redeemed, and the divine passion to redeem it." High authority bids us "Beware when God lets loose a prophet." Beware when God does not let loose a prophet! Ecclesiastical matters are shaken; but much order abides in strength. Of late there has been quick and bold thinking; but we know where we are. This is all preparatory, not final. I see no reason why we could not reconstruct our forms of belief. Such work has been done many times. It can only be done by men in whom the life lives. We have quantities of material: gold, silver, precious stones; and perhaps the rest. But the one foundation standeth sure. We ought to be able to build anew. Perhaps we ought to be willing.

But what the world needs first, and to the end, is God. Not God in the heavens, and in the past, alone. But God here, and ready by "the man whom he hath ordained" to repeat and enlarge the work recorded in Genesis, and many times promised in the New Testament, and to create a man in his own image, with his own heart, a new man in the Son of Man. A revolt against things we do not esteem is of little value unless it leads us from fretting to faith, and brings us to the real life. The appeal to the past needs to reach to the beginning. What did they know who stood near the Apostles which is not in our hands? The years since have added little but experience, with reasoning, defining, asserting. Of the merits of their work we are judges. The New Testament is in our hands and we can read it in English and Greek. We do well to preserve our respect for the Christian thinking which has preceded us. There is wisdom so old that we are children in its presence. Solid, substantial, scholarly, scientific thought distinguishes the Christian centuries, and is nowhere more marked than in the domain of religious truth. We do well to keep before us the learning of other days, and then do our own thinking. These years with their increase of all knowledge must have given light to the truths. It would be strange if religious truth alone were excluded from the learning. It is not that new facts have been added, but new light through life. The truths need to be stated in the terms of the present day, and in the proportions which life now requires. This will keep us in sympathy with the saints, in their feeling if not in its expression; and soon there will be a response in our own hearts. This personal study of the truth we shall not deny to those who inherit our words, and we may ask the same freedom for ourselves.

I have one thing to add in the way of confirmation by personal witness. I have many times said that the Divine force, the Divine life, is now given to men through Jesus Christ, — " I am come that they might have life," — that whosoever consents to receive this from Him shall have it. Is this true? It is an interesting question, even aside from its importance, else I should not set it here. It is more than thirty years since it became my daily life to serve under this belief. As the minister of a large parish, in close connection with the world, and especially with colleges, I have had what seems to me an ample opportunity to determine whether the Divine life is really bestowed in this way. I have now to say to you that I am certain it is bestowed in this way; that whoever opens his heart to the Son of Man, and goes on to obey Him, receives life, with light and strength; a new and living force, which shall make his life true, generous, Divine. This is more than the imparting of a new purpose, a noble desire, a longing for an ideal. It is the giving of life; life for the heart, the conscience, the will; the life which makes a new man. It does not make a full-grown man; but a child rather, whom it brings up into manhood. Bear with me for a moment. In these years which are no longer few I have many times seen the spirit of a man opened quickly before the Son of Man. He has always come in. He comes in whenever the man opens the door. It is as sure as the coming in of the outer air. I have never known it otherwise.

I am willing to trust to this any one whose well-being is of infinite worth in my thought. I am rejoiced when any young man whose heart I have reached goes out from Harvard or Yale with this truth to inspire his life and to be his message to the world. Here it is, so far as I depend upon the warrant of experience, that I have justified myself in writing of the Divine force in the life of the world. The force which reaches a new man, and by repeating this reaches a new world, may well be called Divine. I believe in the Son of Man. Before me He stands, the Man of history, young, erect, brave. He wears no halo but his manly love; with form well defined, the outline sharp against the sky, and the whole being rounded with grace, with the eye clear and gentle as the light, the ear sensitive to a child's thought, a sinner's sigh, the hands strong enough to turn a world, gentle enough to wipe away a tear. He stands the real man, the perfect man, in whom is the fulness of the Divine life, so that the willing man He touches lives, and bears his image and likeness.

If that prophet should ever come his word would be simple, but forcible. He would open the New Testament and read of the Son of Man; and he would call us to devote ourselves to Him; to believe his words, and to take them as the rule of our life; to receive his spirit, that it may control our feeling and thought. He would bid us to trust in Him and in his grace to have eternal life. More than this he would say for enforcement. But the one thing from which he would never swerve is this — that Jesus Christ is the Love of God, in the world redeeming and in heaven enthroned. "I determined not to know anything among you, save Jesus Christ and Him crucified," were the words of a prophet, will be the words of the coming prophet, if he comes. The world will hear and believe, and will find itself and its Creator.

Does all this seem far away? No, this has begun. It was finished that night at Bethlehem, for a divine purpose has its fulfilment in itself. We have seen the end, and now wait for its unfolding. These dull days cannot last much longer. The former times are not better than those which are at hand. We are slowly regaining the spirit of Christianity in our abounding service. Usefulness ranks higher than ever, or anywhere, before. Men are thinking of Christ, talking, writing, reading of Him. He is in the mind. Religious truths are a common theme, and diversity is a hopeful sign of life. Christianity is young and the currents of its life are strong. It was never so great in confidence as in these earnest days. It has broadened with all knowledge. It keeps pace with discovery and geography. It intends to bring the world to its Lord. Its uncompromising faith is pledged to this. It works in the power of the Holy Ghost, the Eternal Spirit. It devotes to this divine end its best treasure, the young life in which to-morrow lives. It will disown itself and its origin when it contracts its design. We have made proof of Christianity, and we know that it can do all that is needed in New England and South America, from Great Britain to Melanesia. David Livingstone and Coleridge Patteson died in full knowledge of its way and work, and an utter belief in it. John Paton among the Christians whom he made from cannibals, by this grace, knows and believes. The knowledge of such men is worth tons of opinion. Theories must make obeisance before results. Things seem to be ready for the spirit of truth and life. In the coming of Christ is the Divine pledge of the completion of his redemptive purpose. That we shall see greater things than these is still his word. He is the living promise, and He will be kept. Not in what men are doing, but in what He is doing, is our confidence. No one versed in his teaching can fail to be brave. Who love Him best, best love their fellow-men, and are bold for their sake. His work is not to be done in a day. It is not the transfer of an outward allegiance; the changing of a banner for the cross. It is deep, in the heart of a man; the overturning of his purpose, the controlling of his life. Every man created anew becomes the minister to his neighbor somewhere. God is in it all. This is his will. Our reliance is on Him. The Son of God is "the transcendent Person of history; and to be transcendent here is to be transcendent everywhere, for religion is the supreme factor in the organizing and the regulating of our personal and collective life." The past inspires us. Lecky had studied the course of the world when he wrote of the three years of Christ's life, that the record of them "has done more to soften and regenerate mankind than all the disquisitions of philosophers, and than all the exhortations of moralists." The historian of morality gave his testimony, that "It was reserved for Christianity to present to the world an ideal character, which through all the changes of eighteen centuries has filled the hearts of men with an impassioned love." It is a glorious consummation to which we look. What is it? The answer is continually upon our lips. The air is hallowed with the promise which answers to our request. We speak in familiar words the end and glory of creation. We say The Lord's Prayer. The end is in it. He taught it, we learned it, long ago. It is the cry of the centuries; in many tongues, in one desire. The child bends at his mother's knee or ever sleep touches his innocent eyes, and lisps as she has told him, "Thy kingdom come." In every college the student as he closes his books to-night and calls home his thoughts, and in manly purpose feels the meaning of his life, finds no truer expression of it than the prayer of his boyhood, "Thy kingdom come."

The priest chants it at the altar. It is spoken by the merchant who has commerce with eternal things; by the lawyer who knows the holiness of law, aware of one Law-giver; the physician whose ministry is health; the man of science whose unfettered thought moves in an open world; the mother, kinswoman with her of Bethlehem, who would extend the sanctity of her home; the soldier without fear and without reproach; the sailor who roams from clime to clime with merchandise which cannot be valued with silver, exchanging thought for thought and adding life to life. "Thy kingdom come," they say. "Thy will be done;" and in the space beneath the heavens the words gather in a cloud of desire; floating quietly above us, illumined, shaped in a holy city with jewelled walls; and under the cloud, here upon the earth, moves on the life, with its word, its touch, its breath; praying, and bringing nearer and more near the longed-for consummation, the crowning of all hope, the passion of the saints, the fulness of life, the new creation perfected, the marriage of the Son of Man to the New Jerusalem. We said it when we were children, we are doing it now, — "Thy kingdom come. Thy will be done."

No better words were found to write upon the wall of Harvard, the mother's blessing for her sons as year by year they go out to do their manly service in the world; against the names of her sons who glorified their learning with devotion, and gave their lives for the country, — there were found no better words than these from one who knew duty and held it more than length of days; "They that be wise shall shine as the brightness of the firmament; and they that turn many to righteousness as the stars for ever and ever."

We are working for this. Many things are ready. The wedding only waits the guests. Blessed is he who summons them! The house is builded and furnished. Our preparation is on a goodly scale. Temples, cathedrals, churches invite worshippers. The kingdom will find its palaces prepared. The stupendous temples of India are ready for the Son of Man. The gods of many arms will give place to Him who held children against his heart, and blessed them there. The walls of Egypt's sanctuaries can quickly be restored. The land of the Nile sheltered Him when He was a child. He will reward it with the goodwill of a man. At Philæ already the cross is cut into the door-post. There has been Christian worship at Luxor, and there might be to-day. Prayer might even now be said among the pillars of Karnak with the majesty of their memory, the heaviness of their silences. I noticed that when the Moslem tore the cross from the door of St. Sophia he left the marks of the nails, and they can go back into their old places. They are to go back. The powers of heaven will restore the cross. It has been needed in these suffering months. It will shed its light upon all the Orient and beyond, circling the globe. It will never fall upon a man whom it cannot help. The light is spreading, slowly. The sun is in it. Let us wait; but let us look. The dawn reaches toward the day. The day will be forever, but the morning will be here. We close our eyes and have the vision:

>   Where faint and far,
>   Along the tingling desert of the sky,
>   Beyond the circle of the conscious hills,
>   Were laid in jasper-stone as clear as glass
>   The first foundations of that new, near Day
>   Which should be builded out of heaven to God.

INDEX.

AGASSIZ, LOUIS.
 his prayer at Penikese . . . 45
ALTRUISM.
 a name for Christian service, 192
ANGELS.
 their place 56
APOSTLES, THE.
 their devotion 245
 the later use of the name . 256
ARYANS.
 their idea of creation . . . 89
ASSOCIATIONS, THE YOUNG MEN'S CHRISTIAN.
 their strength 290
 in colleges 293
 international 293
AURELIUS, MARCUS.
 his character 241
BACON, ROGER.
 his ability 253
 his superstition 253
BIBLE, THE.
 regarded as literature . . 6, 129
 the earliest chapters . 6, 18–22
 harmony with science, 17, 19, 20
 a book of nature 18
 high estimate of man . . . 58
 value of, as authority . . . 126
 the New Testament 132
BRACE, C. L.
 Gesta Christi 250

BRAHMA.
 his time 98
 his teaching 98
BRITAIN.
 early religion of 273
BROOKS, PHILLIPS.
 his testimony 309
BUDDHA.
 his birth 99
 his life 99
 protected from evil 100
 his view of life 100
 Nirvana 100
 his view of man 100
 Buddhism 101, 102
BUSHNELL.
 on the dignity of human nature 62
CALENDAR, THE.
 Dionysian 123
 its relation to Christianity . 123
CALVINISM.
 its strength 317
CASTE.
 in India 99
CATO, THE ELDER.
 his character 241
CAUSATION.
 continuity of 35
CHRIST.
 his birth used in the calendar, 118

INDEX

CHRIST.
- biographies of 126
- in the Old Testament . . . 132
- in the lives of his friends . 133
- in the Book of Acts . . . 133
- known by St. Paul 134
- to be known now 137
- witness of the churches to . 139
- time of his coming 143
- his home at Nazareth . 146, 151
- his childhood 147
- his education 148
- first visit to the Temple . . 149
- his baptism 152
- his first disciples 155
- his temptation 152
- the second Adam 153
- his miracle at Cana 154
- the cleansing of the Temple, 155
- interview with Nicodemus . 155
- with the woman of Samaria, 156
- at Sychar 158
- at the synagogue of Nazareth 158
- his personality 159
- his mission 159, 161
- his transfiguration 160
- his crucifixion 160, 184
- his death 160, 185
- his relation to the Father . 171
    - to men 173
- as the Shepherd 173
- his use of "My" . . . 174, 198
- as the vine 174
- as the Creator 175
- the name Jesus 177
    - Emmanuel . . . 177
    - Christ 177
- his Kingdom 178, 187
- his entrance into Jerusalem, 183
- his teaching 190, 197

CHRIST.
- his teaching of service . . . 192
    - money . . . 193
    - the prodigal, 200
- was the reality 201
- his miracles 202
- required faith 207
- required prayer 212
- required the Sabbath . . . 213
- effects of his life 221
- the power of his Love . . 223
- his confidence in his friends, 225
- the close of his life 239
- present preparation for . . 327

CHRISTIANITY.
- its meaning 136
- to be known now 136
- the spread of 247, 257
- its influence 249, 268
- present condition 261
- organizations 262
- effect of national changes, 270
- proof of its worth . 307-311, 320

CHRISTIANS.
- persecutions of 232
- teaching by the Spirit . . . 238
- their character described . 259
- every one a force 261
- the name 304

CHURCHES.
- their testimony to Christ . 138

CLARK, N. G.
- his testimony to Christianity, 269

CONSCIENCE.
- its witness to God 48

CREATION.
- a new word 9
- the act of creation 9, 33
- eternal 12
- a beginning needed 13

INDEX

CREATION.
    Plato's account of 15
    God's delight in 16
    various accounts of 21
    spiritual in its origin 26
    of man 26, 30
DEATH.
    its meaning and place . . . 89
DESIGN.
    argument from 24
    Asa Gray on 44
DIONYSIUS.
    his calendar 123
DISCIPLES, THE.
    their devotion to Christ . . 222
    their fidelity 228
DISOBEDIENCE.
    its beginning 81
    reason for 86
DUTY.
    the ground of 65
    love is 67
    under evolution 69
    Hooker on 74
EDWARDS, JONATHAN.
    his consciousness of God . . 40
ELIOT, C. W.
    interest of universities in religious institutions . . 297
EMERSON, R. W.
    on duty 74
ENGLAND.
    influence of 286
ERSKINE, THOMAS.
    his consciousness of God . . 41
FETICHISM.
    defined 113
FRANCIS, SAINT, OF ASSISI.
    his preaching to birds . . . 72
GOD.
    in the beginning . . . 6, 8, 11

GOD.
    fellowship in his being . . . 9
    self-revelation of 12
    his relation to creation . 14, 35
    a supreme moment with . . 16
    the only life 34, 63
    universal idea of 43
    witness of conscience . . . 48
    not the author of evil . . . 91
GRAY, ASA.
    the design in nature 44
HINDOOS.
    Maurice on 102
HITCHCOCK, R. D.
    on superstition in religion, 107
    on the conquests of Christianity, 315
HOLMES, O. W.
    on suffering in the world . 306
HOLY SPIRIT, THE.
    at Pentecost 228
    his place and work 229
HOOKER, RICHARD.
    on duty 74
HUMMING-BIRD.
    the life of 32
INDIA.
    the land 98
    Brahmans 98
    caste 99
    Buddhism 99, 101
    has no light for the world . 104
JAPAN.
    Buddhism in 103
JESUS CHRIST.
    the name 177
JOHN THE BAPTIST.
    his coming 144
    his preaching 145
JOWETT, BENJAMIN.
    on the state of the world . 243

INDEX

KINGDOM OF HEAVEN.
  described 178, 187
LECKY, W. E. H.
  on the king's touch 253
LIFE.
  continuity of 11
  forms of 13, 26
  first living creature 20
  mystery of 32
  of a bird 32
  the only life 34, 63
  lower and higher 34, 72
LIVINGSTONE, DAVID.
  a witness to Christ . . 138, 323
LOVE.
  in creation 16
  called for man 27
  interprets life 31
  is duty 67
MAN.
  the first 26
  a living soul 30, 69
  his creation 30
  made religion possible . . . 33
  his double relation . . . 34, 53
  lightly regarded 57
  dignity of 62
  to be like his maker 64
  his Edenic happiness . . 68, 70
  lame or halting creature . . 68
  connected with lower forms of
    life 71
  transition from obedience, 76, 79, 85
  his slow ascent 77
  his "fall up" 80
  in the garden of Eden . . . 80
  out of the garden 88
  the problem of recovery . . 95
MAURICE, F. D.
  his consciousness of God . . 41

MAURICE, F. D.
  on the Hindoos 102
MIRACLES.
  at Cana 154
  described 204
  on the lame man at the Temple 231
MISSIONS.
  essential to Christianity . . 259
  their forces 262
  their results 272
  to Britain 274
  well established 288
  still needed 295
MULFORD, E.
  on the belief in God 41
MULLER, G.
  his orphanage 267
NANSEN, FRIDTJOF.
  reasoning from driftwood . 94
NATURE.
  its permanent meaning . . . 16
  its early records 23
NAZARETH.
  its synagogue visited . . . 158
NELSON, HORATIO.
  signal at Trafalgar 225
NICODEMUS.
  his interview with Christ . 155
OBEDIENCE.
  the nature of 67
  the ground of 66
  transition from 76, 79
PALESTINE.
  a fitting place for the life of
    Christ 142
PARSEES.
  their stories of creation . . . 90
PATON, J. G.
  his witness to Christianity, 324

INDEX

PATTESON, J. C.
  his witness to Christianity . 323
PAUL, SAINT.
  a witness to Christ 134
  his conversion 232
  his ministry 233
  his authority 237
PEABODY, A. P.
  on the person of Christ . . 172
  his testimony 308
PENIKESE.
  Agassiz's prayer on 45
PENTECOST, DAY OF.
  its importance 227
PETER, SAINT.
  his miracle at the Temple, 231
PLATO.
  describes creation 15
  on the soul 39
PLINY.
  on the spread of Christianity, 247
PRAYER.
  a part of Christianity . . . 212
  the Lord's Prayer 325
PROPHET.
  the one coming 318
RAMABAI, PUNDITA.
  on the women of India . . 110
RELIGION.
  separate from preaching . . . 3
  reality of 5
  variety in 5
  confesses a supreme will . . . 7
  is personal 7
  source of 8
  universal 8
  without science 13
  became possible 33
  demanded by men 94

RELIGIONS.
  of the world 103
  insist on morality 105
  reveal man 105
  superstition in 106
  insufficient 108
  a common principle in . . . 112
REPUBLIC, THE AMERICAN.
  formation of 282
  its influence 286
ROBERTSON, F. W.
  it is right to do right 66
SABBATH, THE.
  a part of Christianity . . . 213
SAMARIA.
  Christ at the well of . . . 156
SCIENCE.
  without religion 13
  confirmed by the Bible . 17, 20
  opposition to 251
  formed by Christianity . . 252
SERPENT, THE.
  in the garden 83
SOUL, THE.
  what it is 33
  is the man 36, 69
  origin of 36
  Plato on 39
SPENCER, HERBERT.
  on the being of God 42
STEPHEN, SAINT.
  his martyrdom 233
STORRS, R. S.
  his lectures 249
SUPERSTITION.
  in religions 106
  Hitchcock on 107
TEMPTATION, THE.
  in the garden of Eden . . . 87
  not of God 91
  temptation of Christ . . . 152

TRADITION.
   source of 19
TRUTH.
   independent of form 4
VIRCHOW, PROFESSOR.
   on life 11
WALKER, J.
   the gospel of encouragement, 59
   on the person of Christ . . 172
   his testimony 309
WINTHROP, J.
   on the design of the Puritans 284

WOOLSEY, THEODORE.
   his testimony 307
WORSHIP.
   by the Zuni Indians . . . 113
   of the heavens 114
YOUNG MEN'S CHRISTIAN ASSOCIATIONS.
   their purpose and strength . 290
   in colleges 293
   international 293
ZUNI INDIANS.
   their worship 113

www.ingramcontent.com/pod-product-compliance
Lightning Source LLC
Chambersburg PA
CBHW031853220426
43663CB00006B/606